IMAGES
of America
SANTA SUSANA

SIMI VALLEY AERIAL VIEW, C. 1986. Within a span of 25 years, Simi Valley was transformed from a rural farming district to a bedroom community exceeding 100,000 residents. The 1940 census for Simi Valley showed 3,106 residents. Ten years later, the figure was 5,150 residents, and in 1959, the number almost doubled to 10,998. Growth continued at an enormous pace until there was no room for further development except in the surrounding hills. Santa Susana includes all the area east from present-day Tapo Canyon Road to the Santa Susana Pass. (Courtesy Holly Huff.)

ON THE COVER: The Simi Hotel in the 1890s was the scene of constant activity as potential buyers for land came and went by stagecoach, horse and buggy, and wagon to survey the property offered by the Simi Land and Water Company. At the time, the cost per acre for land was between $20 and $100 depending on location, number of acres purchased, and proximity to the Arroyo Simi water supply. (Courtesy Simi Valley Historical Society and Museum.)

IMAGES *of America*
SANTA SUSANA

Bill Appleton
Simi Valley Historical Society

Copyright © 2009 by Bill Appleton, Simi Valley Historical Society
ISBN 978-1-5316-4624-0

Published by Arcadia Publishing
Charleston, South Carolina

Library of Congress Control Number: 2009921925

For all general information contact Arcadia Publishing at:
Telephone 843-853-2070
Fax 843-853-0044
E-mail sales@arcadiapublishing.com
For customer service and orders:
Toll-Free 1-888-313-2665

Visit us on the Internet at www.arcadiapublishing.com

"SANTA SUSANA. YA-TAH-HEY." This image of Chief Flying Cloud was taken in 1941 in the Santa Susana Mountains to promote a Western film directed by Raoul Walsh. Director Walsh made Santa Susana his home in 1968 after he retired from a prolific 50-year motion picture career that started in the silent-film era and continued into the era of television. (Courtesy of Mary Walsh.)

Contents

Acknowledgments		6
Introduction		7
1.	Early Santa Susana History	9
2.	Oil, Land, and Southern Pacific Company	33
3.	Santa Susana Township	51
4.	Tapo Citrus and Walnut Growers Associations	65
5.	Santa Susana Airport	75
6.	Corriganville Movie Ranch	85
7.	Susana Knolls and Santa Susana Field Laboratory	97
8.	Grandma Prisbrey's Bottle Village	107
9.	Communes, Cults, and the WKFL	115
Bibliography		127

Acknowledgments

First and foremost, I would like to thank my wife, Linda, for her never-ending support. Without her encouragement and understanding, this book would never have been possible.

The author wishes to express thanks and appreciation to Patricia Havens, museum director for the Strathearn Historical Park, for her many years of support, encouragement, and access to her files and archives. Additionally, I extend thanks to the current and former members of the board of directors of the Simi Valley Historical Society and Museum for their interest and encouragement along with Lynn Sacks who was always most helpful.

Many thanks go to the following individuals who provided information, photographs, documents, support, and other articles that lent to the research of Santa Susana: my mother and father, Mr. and Mrs. William H. Appleton; Pat Berry; Pat Bosquet; Howard Bowman; Nikki Broiles; Charlie Brooks; Juanita Gillibrand Brooks; Woodrow Clary; Tom Corrigan; Bob Crinklaw; Bob Crowell; Ruth Harrington Dempsey; William Ehrheart; Barbara Foster Elliot; Kathy Ervin; Betty Lou Evans; Lorene Foster; Claudine Fowler; Ken Garges; Lorraine Sailer Hammerlee; Ross Harrington; Neil Havens; Norm Havins; Joe Hitch; Merle Hollis; John Hollis; Linda Fincham Hollinger; Holly Huff; Helen Jackson; John Johnson; Erika Kaiser; John McCarthy; Mary Janet Meyer; Vicki Mitchell; Esther Mosesso; Sharon Ruedy; Maxine Hughes Smith; Grace Werner Sorrells; Ruby Taylor Stevens; Shawn Sutherland; Eleanor Taylor; Mary Walsh; Jack Wilson; and Gene Wurtz.

For information and photographs about the Santa Susana Railroad Depot, I thank Tom Bergh and Curt Osterhaudt. I extend special acknowledgement to Jerry Schneider and Larry Parson for photographs from the Corriganville Movie Ranch. Thanks and recognition goes to Joanne Johnson for information and photographs about Tressa Prisbrey along with Kathy LaForce, Drew Kennedy, and Daniel Paul. For photographs and information about the Santa Susana Field Laboratory, I would like to thank Jerry Blackburn of the Aerospace Legacy Foundation and Rocketdyne Archives. Special thanks go to Bob Daggs of Impressive Photos for his assistance providing digital scanning and especially to Jerry Roberts at Arcadia Publishing for his guiding support to make *Santa Susana* a reality. Most of the photographs are from the collections of the author and the Simi Valley Historical Society and Museum.

INTRODUCTION

Today as you approach Tapo Street from Los Angeles Avenue, there are two monuments adjacent to the railroad tracks that read "Santa Susana Town Center." Placed during the Tapo Street revitalization, this is passing acknowledgement to the town of Santa Susana that began when the Southern Pacific Company built a railroad depot in 1903 and named it after the neighboring mountains, *Sierra de Santa Susanna*.

The name Santa Susana can be traced to Rome and a Catholic church that was built in the 4th century. The church was dedicated in 590 AD to St. Susanna who was beheaded and martyred. There is also a town located on the Costa Brava in the Catalonia region of northeast Spain and named in honor of the saint.

The town of Santa Susana had been in place almost 70 years when a group of business people decided to incorporate the three small towns of Simi Valley. Forty years ago, the fate of Santa Susana was decided by a special election. The question put to the voters was whether they wanted to incorporate and become a city and if so, what should the city be named. Voters had two choices: Simi Valley or Santa Susana.

By a 2:1 margin, the voters elected to become a city, and they chose Simi Valley for the name. On October 10, 1969, the City of Simi Valley was officially incorporated and just like that, it became the third largest city in Ventura County.

The town name Santa Susana seemingly disappeared overnight. But the stories and events of the people who shaped Santa Susana live on through the history of the area as presented in this publication.

*Readers should note that the spelling of Susana/Susanna uses both the single-"N" and double-"N" variations in this text. At times in the first two chapters, the longer variation is used to pay tribute to the early history of the area and specific names. The shorter version became accepted in later years.

SIMI HOTEL FROM LOS ANGELES AVENUE. The Simi Hotel, with its distinctive Queen Anne–style and red gabled roof, was the first building of major consequence to be constructed in Simi Valley. The hotel was built on a knoll about where the Simi Valley High School football and track field at Cochran and Stow Streets presently intersect.

One

EARLY SANTA SUSANA HISTORY

Prior to the mission period, the Chumash Indians inhabited Simi Valley. Three settlements have been identified: *Ta'apu*, from which the word Tapo evolved; *Shimiyi*, which became shortened to the word Simí; and a third village, *Quimisac* or *Kimishax*. The village of *Ta'apu* was the largest of the three settlements, located 2 miles up the present-day Tapo Canyon. The village of *Ta'apu* had a resident chief named Zalasuit who was later baptized as Salvador at Mission San Fernando in 1804. Three known Chumash from the village of *Ta'apu* survived into the mission period: Tiburcio Cayo (1793–1844), Leopoldo Cuticucagele (1799–1865), and Maria del Pilar Siguisalmeulgel (1807–1860).

The land known today as El Rancho Simi was officially registered during the mission period as San José de Nuestra Señora de Altagracia y Simí. Santiago Pico was granted permission to occupy the 113,000-acre parcel in 1795 by the king of Spain when he was 63 years of age. It was essentially a "grazing permit" for the old soldier from Mexico and his family. By 1832, El Rancho Simi was sold to Don José de la Guerra y Noriega. Around this same time, a smaller body of land called El Rancho Tapo became known as a separate place within El Rancho Simi. This tract of land consisted of about 14,400 acres.

In 1860, the coastal stage of the Overland Mail Company was routed through Simi Valley to establish a path for mail delivery between Los Angeles and San Francisco. A primitive road that followed an old Chumash trail was cut just wide enough to allow a wagon to traverse the Santa Susanna Mountains from the San Fernando Valley into Simi. The new road over the Santa Susanna Pass was completed by April 1861. At the foot of Twilight Canyon where the west portal of the present-day Santa Susana tunnel begins, a stage stop called Mountain Station was established.

By 1865, El Rancho Simi became the property of the Philadelphia and California Petroleum Company, an eastern oil syndicate that purchased the land grant from the de la Guerra family for oil exploration. This marked the arrival of the first Americans, including, in 1872, Charles Emerson Hoar, who developed the Humming Bird Nest Ranch at the east end of the valley.

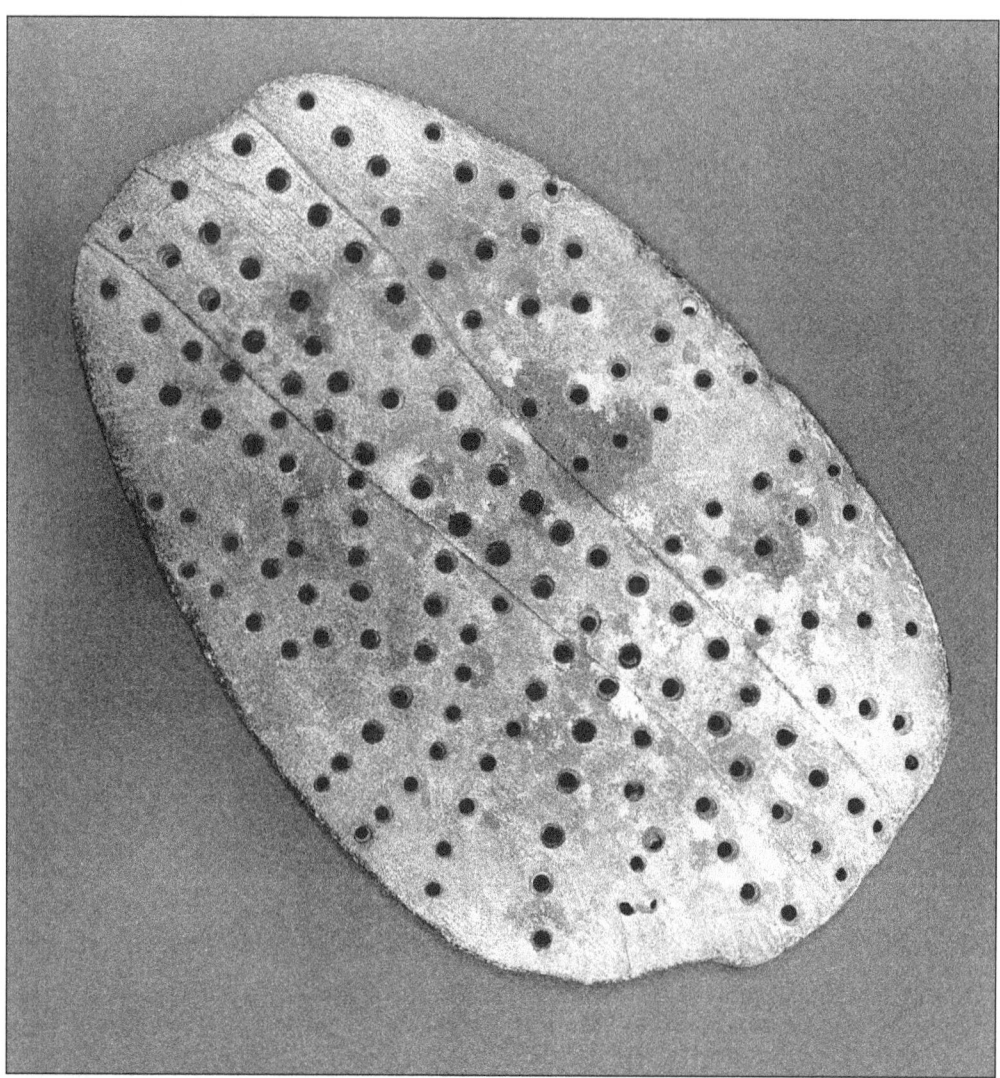

CHUMASH EFFIGY TABLET. This unusual artifact was discovered by Philip Walton Gillibrand in Tapo Canyon around 1900. Believed to be a type of Chumash Indian calendar, the object measures 10 inches long and 6.25 inches wide. Gillibrand found the stone near his parent's house at the top of a hill.

BURRO FLATS PAINTED CAVE. One of the better Chumash Indian pictograph caves in Simi Valley was discovered on the *Putrero del Burro* (Burro Flats area) of the Santa Susanna Mountains around the turn of the 20th century. This photograph taken in the 1950s shows a North American Aviation employee inside the pictograph cave.

CHUMASH PICTOGRAPH DETAIL. This close-up view shows the central portion of the Burro Flats Painted Cave pictograph near the Santa Susana Field Laboratory. Anthropologists believe the cave was used as a winter solstice observatory and that the drawings celebrate the solstice or "return of the sun." Some experts believe the paintings date to 500 AD.

José Antonio de la Guerra y Noriega (1779–1858). Don José purchased El Rancho Simi from the Pico family in 1832. His land holdings in the area had all but diminished to El Rancho Tapo by 1877 when it was sold to Abraham Bernheim for a debt. De la Guerra was born at Novales, Santander, Spain, and came to Mexico where he joined the frontier army. De La Guerra later served at Santa Barbara and became commandant of the presidio in 1827. He was popularly known as El Capitán.

Tapo Adobe Ruins, 1904. This photograph of the old de la Guerra adobe grounds was used in a report by a hydraulic engineer studying the water and irrigation possibilities in the Tapo area. The property had been recently purchased by the Patterson Ranch Company, and the picture shows what remained of the old fruit orchard and two-story adobe that once served as the hacienda owned by José de la Guerra.

DE LA GUERRA ADOBE, C. 1900. The José de la Guerra adobe was most likely constructed between 1820 and 1830 and was used by the family for several decades. Most adobes were single-level constructions, and this example of a two-story building was unique.

MEXICAN SHEEPSHEARERS, 1890s. A group of Mexican sheepshearers pose for a Garden City Photo Company photographer. In the 1840s, José de la Guerra used El Rancho Simi mostly for raising cattle, although he did keep a small number of sheep in the Tapo Canyon area. It was not until the 1870s that large-scale sheep ranching began in Simi Valley.

TIBURCIO VASQUEZ (1835–1875). Vasquez was the last of the famous Mexican banditos. His travels reached into Simi Valley, and Flora DeNure, wife of Delos DeWolf DeNure, wrote about an encounter she had with the legendary bandit in the 1870s late one night at the foot of the Santa Susanna Pass at Larry's stage stop.

SIMI STAGE ROAD, 1887. The Simi Stage Road coming down from Larry's stage stop at the foot of the pass followed what is now Smith Road as it passed through the Roblaro. This view taken by photographer C. F. Shaffner shows a section of that road at the time the Simi Hotel was being built in 1887.

COAST STAGE LINE TIME TABLE, 1871. The second stage stop out of Los Angeles was Mountain Station, also called Larry's stage stop. It was located 33 miles from Los Angeles in Simi Valley, required five hours of travel time, and cost $4 for the fare. Note the third stage stop, named Sime [sic], which was located near Tierra Rejada Road.

GILROY and LOS ANGELES.
COAST STAGE LINE.

W. G. ROBERTS, Agent, office 208 Montgomery street, San Francisco.
General Agent, W. BUCKLEY, San Jose, California.
Local Agents: Jos. KNOWLTON, Jr., Gilroy; WM. BALCH, San Juan; CHRS. HAMEL, Natividad; L. C. Bortick, Plato Ranch; CHAS. KNOWLTON, Paso Robles Springs; J. C. ORTEGA, San Luis Obispo; ELI RUNDELL, Santa Barbara; J. WOOLFSON, San Buenaventura; GEO. M. FALL, Los Angeles.
Stage leaves Gilroy daily at 12 M. Stage leaves Los Angeles daily at 6 A. M.

From Gilroy To Los Angeles.			TOWNS May 18th, 1871.	See Page.	From Los Angeles To Gilroy.		
Fare.	Hours	Miles.			Miles.	Hours	Fare.
$ 0.00	0	0	Dep......Gilroy......Arr.	161	366	58	
1.50	2	12	..........San Juan..........		354		
2.50	4	24	..........Natividad..........		342		
4.00	6	38	..........Utz Station..........		328		
5.50	8	52	..........Salinas River..........		314		
8.50	11	76	..........Last Chance..........		290		
10.00	13	92	..........San Antonio..........		274		
12.00	15	107	..........Plato Ranch..........		259		
14.00	17	121	..........Nacimento..........		245		
15.00	19	136	......Paso Robles Hot Springs.....		230		
16.00	22	150	..........San Margarita..........		216		
16.00	25	164	..........San Luis Obispo.........	174	202	36	
17.50	28	180	..........Arroyo Grande..........		186		
17.50	31	196	..........Zury Station..........		170		
17.50	33	214	..........Foxens..........		152		
17.50	35	228	..........Ballard's..........		138		
17.50	37	243	..........San Marcus..........		123		
17.20	40	257	..........McCaffery's..........		109		
17.50	41	265	..........Santa Barbara.........	174	101	15	
18.00	44	280	..........Rincon..........		86		
18.00	47	293	..........San Buenaventura.....		73	11	
20.00	49	306	..........Santa Clara Valley........		60		
20.00	51	320	..........Sime..........		46		
20.00	53	333	..........Mountain Station........		33	5	
20.00	56	350	..........El Cino............		16	2	
20.00	58	366	Arr......Los Angeles......Dep.	164	0	0	

Connections.

At Gilroy, connects with cars of S. F. & S. J. R. R. for San Francisco.
At San Juan, connects with stages for Watsonville and Santa Cruz, New Idria Castroville, Salinas City, and Monterey.
At San Luis Obispo, connects with stage for San Simeon.
At Los Angeles, connects with stages for San Diego, Fort Yuma and Tucson San Bernardino, La Paz and Clear Creek.

GILROY and SULPHUR SPRINGS.
CAVANA'S STAGE LINE.

Stages leave Gilroy daily at 12.30 P. M.; arrive at Canada de Los Assos at 2.30 P. M.; distance 8 miles; fare $1.00; arrive at Hot Sulphur Springs at 3.30 P. M.; distance 15 miles; through fare $2.00. Returning, leave Hot Springs at 8 A. M.; arrive at Gilroy at 11 A. M. Connect at Gilroy with stages for Santa Cruz, Watsonville and Monterey, and cars for San Francisco.

SIMI STAGE ROAD, 2005. This photograph of the old Simi Stage Road was taken in 2005 just after the big fire that burned through the Santa Susanna Mountains. It shows the old road is still defined and traversable leading up Twilight Canyon from the west portal of the railroad tunnel to the crest of the pass.

THOMAS ALEXANDER SCOTT (1823–1881). Colonel Scott was president of the Pennsylvania Railroad when he took ownership of the 96,000-acre El Rancho Simi in 1865. Scott served in the Union army during the Civil War and had extensive knowledge of rail and transportation systems. Scott met the young Thomas Bard during the Civil War and hired him to manage his business interests in California where disputes concerning land titles were a full-time job.

ROBLARO SHEEP CAMP, 1887. This early photograph taken by Los Angeles photographer C. F. Shaffner shows Charles Emerson Hoar, Bud and Frank Taylor, and Juan Pucillo at their sheep camp on the Roblaro. Hoar smokes his pipe in the horse cart while the Taylor brothers wait for Juan Pucillo to prepare a meal on the campfire.

THOMAS ROBERT BARD (1841–1915). Thomas Bard was born in Chambersburg, Pennsylvania. Early in 1865, Bard came to Ventura County to take charge of Thomas Scott's business affairs. In 1871, Bard built the wharf at Hueneme and helped establish the town site known today as Port Hueneme. After the death of Colonel Scott in 1881, Bard was appointed administrator of his California estate to liquidate his land holdings. Thomas Bard served as a California senator from 1900 to 1905.

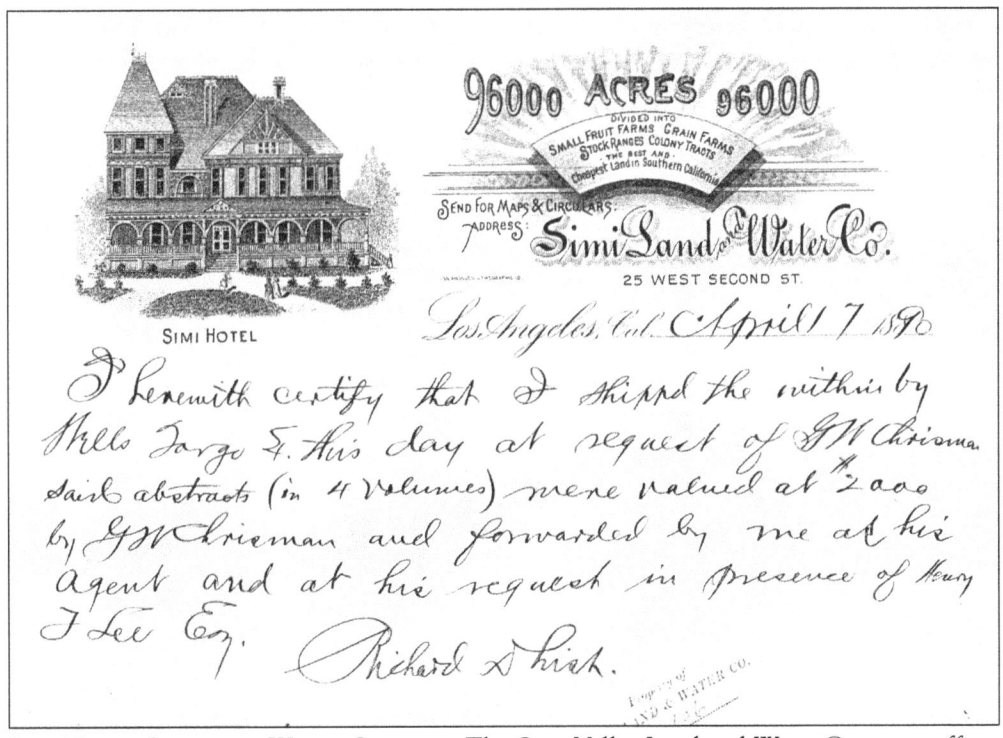

SIMI VALLEY LAND AND WATER COMPANY. The Simi Valley Land and Water Company offices were located in Los Angeles and managed by Robert W. Poindexter. There were seven men on the board of directors headed by Thomas R. Bard, who was also the majority stockholder in the corporation. By August 1890, they had sold 68,000 acres of the original survey of 96,000 acres.

SIMI SHEEP RANCH, 1887. This photograph shows one of the sheepfolds operated by Charles Emerson Hoar (seated in the surrey) at the east end of the valley in 1887. Shown standing are Charley McCoy (left), manager of the Simi Hotel, and a man believed to be Marshall Bates. Hoar ran about 6,000 head of sheep on the land he rented from Thomas Bard.

PATTERSON RANCH HOG PEN. It is feeding time for the hogs in Tapo Canyon. The Patterson Ranch was located on the same property that was once owned by José de la Guerra. It was purchased in 1903 with the northern portion of the 14,000-acre ranch used for raising stock, grain, beans, and beets and the southern portion for citrus, walnut, and apricot ranches.

SIMI STAGE DRIVER, JOE HORNER. This photograph shows the four-horse stagecoach that made runs between the Simi Hotel and San Fernando in the 1890s. Joe Horner is the driver coming down the old stage road from the Santa Susanna Pass. Horner got his first job after coming to Simi in 1888 from Charley McCoy, who ran the Simi Hotel for the Simi Valley Land and Water Company.

HUMMING BIRD NEST RANCH ADOBE, 1887. This is the only known photograph of the adobe at the Humming Bird Nest Ranch when it was occupied by Charles Emerson Hoar. It shows the adobe with a wooden roof, protruding stove pipe, whitewashed walls, and an adjoining structure on the south side added by Hoar. The property had a good spring of water and 10 acres of rich soil on fairly level land.

JOHN S. HARE ON PATTERSON RANCH. John Hare became the resident manager of the Patterson Ranch in Tapo Canyon in 1903. He came at a young age from Poland with Helena Modjeska, the famous Polish actress, to her estate in Santa Ana where he studied agriculture and horticulture. Later he joined the American Beet Sugar Company in Oxnard and then moved to the Tapo to oversee farming operations, which included raising cattle, hogs, sheep, grain, beans, and beets.

SIMI HOTEL. Visitors prepare to leave the Simi Hotel for a sightseeing tour around Simi Valley. Janet Scott Cameron noted, "A regular schedule was followed. Mr. McCoy took them in his surrey on a sightseeing tour to the Humming Bird's Nest 2 miles to the east where Mr. Hoar showed them his fruits and flowers and vegetables as well as his 'look-out' at the foot of his favorite rock, the Santa Susana, from where one could see the whole length of the valley. Next, they visited the old de la Guerra adobe up on the Tapo with its gardens and orchards and vineyards."

HOLT COMBINE HARVESTER. This photograph shows a Holt Company combine harvester cutting grain on the Tapo Alto Ranch in the 1890s. Edward Clayton Gillibrand stands atop the big machine that required about 30 horses and mules to pull it through the fields.

GRAIN HARVEST ON LOS ANGELES AVENUE. Wagonloads of grain harvested from the Gillibrand Ranch are shown in this scene on Los Angeles Avenue in Santa Susana adjacent to the railroad depot. The building in the distant background is the Santa Susana School that was constructed in 1902 on the west side of South Tapo Street.

EDWARD CLAYTON GILLIBRAND. "Gillie," as he was called by his friends, takes a break from cattle ranching to light a cigarette. Gillibrand came to Simi Valley in 1889 and purchased the 6,000-acre Rancho Tapo Alto with his brother-in-law, Jack Hesketh. Gillibrand came to California from Timperly, Cheshire, England, where his father was head of a silk and cotton spinning firm.

GILLIBRAND RANCH COWBOYS. "Sage" Cornett wrote about California cowboys: "I was allowed to go to the spring and fall roundups. This gave me a chance to work with the best cowboys and horsemen I have ever seen in all my travels. These men were more interested in their horses than anything else. These horses were all from Spanish mares crossed with thoroughbreds, standard breeds, and Arabians. These well-bred horses had more wind than jack rabbits."

SIMI HOTEL, C. 1890. The Simi Hotel was designed by San Francisco architect Joseph Cather Newsome and built in 1887. At a cost of about $12,000, the 26-room hotel boasted a large reception area, a 20-foot-by-40-foot dining room, nine sleeping rooms, and quarters and storage on the third floor for the hotel staff. Charles McCoy became resident manager of the establishment with his wife, Nellie, who ran the kitchen.

CHARLEY ASHBY. Ashby reads the Sunday *Los Angeles Times* in front of his lodging place on the Tapo Alto Ranch. This makeshift style of living quarters where a wooden floor was used in combination with a tent to provide sleeping quarters for ranch hands was not uncommon.

ELLEN LELAND GILLIBRAND. This youthful portrait was taken of Ellen Leland Gillibrand in England prior to her coming to California. Leland married Edward Clayton Gillibrand in 1886 and shortly after, she and her husband set sail for America. The couple first settled in Virginia City, later moved to Lancaster, and came to Simi Valley in 1889.

LOADING HAY, TAPO ALTA RANCH. Jack Haigh (left) and Edward Clayton Gillibrand (on haystack) gather a load of hay on the Tapo Alto Ranch. Gillibrand's three boys are at the left side. Jack Haigh, like Gillibrand, came to California from England and had spent four years as a gaucho in Argentina.

"Bo" and "Toe" Gillibrand. This Cabinet Card photograph taken in Ventura in the 1890s shows two of the Gillibrand boys: Ralph Leyland, left, and Philip Walton, right. They were given the nicknames "Toe" and "Bo," which stuck with them for the rest of their lives as they continued ranching on their father's land in Tapo Canyon.

Steer Branding, Tapo Alta Ranch. Cowboys brand a steer in the roundup corral of the Tapo Alto Ranch. Edward Clayton Gillibrand (standing) assists his brother Arthur as he applies the brand with a stamp iron. Note in the background that the corral posts fashioned from newly cut willow have taken root and sprouted new growth.

FAMILY OUTING ON THE TAPO, C. 1900. Family members of Napoleon Bonaparte Cornett, Will Kier, Ed Patterson, and Maroni Stones gather for a picture at an outing in Tapo Canyon. Johnny Baldwin is riding the horse at the left, and Frank Pyle is on the horse to the right.

TAPO ALTO RANCH. Here are the cowboy quarters on the Tapo Alto Ranch. This photograph taken at the Gillibrand bunkhouse shows the simplicity of the times: neatly hung tacks, a few cowboy mementos, the *Los Angeles Times* Sunday edition newspaper, and a dog curled up asleep on the bunk bed.

STEER BRANDING ON THE PATTERSON RANCH. Three cowboys working for the Patterson Ranch in Tapo Canyon brand a steer on the open range in the 1890s. In this photograph taken by A. M. Pollock of the Garden City Photo Company, the photographer used an elevated tripod and camera. Pollock designed a ladder that attached to his horse-drawn wagon that was capable of a 25-foot elevation for his 8-inch-by-10-inch-view camera when photographing landscapes.

ARROYO SIMI, 1887. This photograph of the Arroyo Simi near the Susana Knolls was taken in 1887 at about the time the Simi Hotel was being built. Advertisers in the eastern newspapers highly misrepresented the amount of water in Simi Valley. One writer wrote, "Bordering the maps, there were pictures of boating and fishing parties along the Simi Creek, this notwithstanding the fact that the Arroyo was dry for the greater part of the year."

EILEEN HAIGH, 1916. Eileen was the daughter of Grace and Henry Haigh who came to Simi Valley from Parkgate, Cheshire, England, in the 1890s and relocated in Tapo Canyon. There were very few conveniences in Simi Valley in the early days, but Eileen never forgot her English heritage and always dressed in fashionable attire.

SAMUEL MILLER WOODSON EASLEY. Easley moved to Sycamore Canyon (present-day site of the Brandeis-Bardin Institute) in 1883 and started the first school in Simi Valley. Easley, born in Missouri, migrated across the Great Plains and settled near present-day San Jose where he married and taught school. The family then moved to San Buenaventura where Easley became the first acting Ventura County clerk when the county formed in 1872. This photograph shows Easley in his bee apiary.

FRANK CORNETT, SANTA SUSANNA PASS. The Cornett family came to Ventura County from Missouri and settled in Simi in 1884. Napoleon Bonaparte Cornett and his wife had six boys and one daughter, and his son Frank became an expert horseman who worked with stock in Mexico and every territory and state west of Kansas City. His book, *Recollections of a Pioneer Cowboy*, provides some of the earliest accounts of the first Americans in Simi Valley.

GILLIBRAND RANCH COWBOYS. This image by Garden City Photo Company shows how a steer is roped and readied for branding. Edward Clayton Gillibrand is the mounted rider (second from the left), and other family members and ranch hands observe the demonstration. This card was most likely in a series of photographic illustrations published to show city residents what life was like on the cattle ranches surrounding Los Angeles.

Maroni Stones. Maroni Stones came to Simi Valley in 1884 from Utah and first lived in the de la Guerra adobe where he was foreman for the Burch and Berry Ranch. This tintype portrait shows him as a young man in the 1860s. Stones was considered to be very adept with a water witch, and he drilled artesian wells for many of the newcomers to the valley.

Tapo Canyon Homestead, 1915. The Haigh family homestead was located in Tapo Canyon under an oak tree. Eileen (standing in doorway) was the daughter of Grace and Henry Haigh who came to ranch in the Tapo area of Simi Valley from England in the 1890s and had six children.

ROAD OUT OF TAPO CANYON. John Sparhawk Appleton took this picture of his father and mother sitting in a buggy on the road leading out of Tapo Canyon after a visit with the Gillibrand family. Lt. Charles F. Appleton, a Civil War veteran, and wife, Mary, had come from West Newbury, Massachusetts, to California to visit their son and his family in the summer of 1908.

TAYLOR'S THRESHING OUTFIT, 1890S. Before the introduction of the Holt Company combine harvester, a large number of men, wagons, horses, mules, and other equipment were needed to cut the grain and transport it to the stationary harvester that did the threshing. This photograph shows "Bud" Taylor's big threshing outfit consisting of over 40 men and 20 horses and mules.

UNIDENTIFIED HUNTER ON BURRO. The foothills of the Santa Susanna Mountains were known for their abundance of dove, quail, rabbits, and an occasional deer. The early residents took advantage of the local wildlife to supplement their food supply. This early resident has his shotgun, frying pan, and bedroll and is about to embark on a hunting trip to see if he can rustle up some grub.

CHARLES EMERSON HOAR. Photographer John Sparhawk Appleton took this picture of Hoar while he was tending to his strawberry patch on August 7, 1907. Hoar moved from the Humming Bird Nest Ranch at the east end of the valley some years earlier to his Royal Avenue Ranch, where he died in 1912 after 42 years of ranching in Simi Valley.

Two

OIL, LAND, AND SOUTHERN PACIFIC COMPANY

The growth of Santa Susana during the first decade of 1900 was largely a result of three factors: the location of the Southern Pacific Railroad depot, discovery of oil on El Rancho Tapo, and the first business constructed near the depot. As drilling and blasting of "the Great Tunnel" through the Santa Susana Mountains neared completion, the Southern Pacific Company selected a location just east of Tapo Street in 1903 for the train depot. They named the train stop Santa Susana, after the mountains at the east end of Simi Valley. The Southern Pacific Company used the double-"N" spelling of Susanna on the depot sign facing west and the single-"N" spelling of Susana on the sign facing east. This spelling dilemma has perplexed people ever since.

Oil production in Tapo Canyon began in 1910 when the Scarab Oil Company drilled two wells and struck oil on one at 2,600 feet. The well opened with production of 300 barrels of oil per day. A pipeline was soon built down to the Southern Pacific depot where storage tanks were located. Later in 1916, Edward Doheny purchased 7,500 acres of land in the Tapo District and paid $110,000 for the property and $250,000 for the oil rights. A year later, he bought an additional 3,000 acres from the Patterson Ranch Company. Oil production and exploration continued over the years, and as late as 1953, a new well was discovered that began producing over 600 barrels a day.

Horace Crinklaw and his wife established the first business in Santa Susana in 1909 when they built a general merchandise store directly across Los Angeles Avenue from the railroad depot. By 1914, the town of Santa Susana contained a total of eight buildings—four of which were built by Crinklaw. The other four included the Santa Susana schoolhouse, Southern Pacific depot, the Southern Pacific Warehouse, and a blacksmith shop on North Tapo Street. This was the beginning of the Santa Susana township.

EVA AND HORACE CRINKLAW. Eva Mahan and Horace Crinklaw were married in 1883 at the Springville church near present-day Camarillo. They reared five children, and after years of developing their business interests in Santa Susana, tragedy struck the family in 1942 when both Eva and Horace were killed in their car by a passenger train at the Erringer Road crossing.

FIRST SANTA SUSANNA STORE, 1910. The Crinklaw General Merchandise Store was located directly across Los Angeles Avenue from the Southern Pacific Railroad depot. It was the first store built in Santa Susana (note the double-"N" spelling of the town) and later housed the post office, which was first located in the train depot. Horace Crinklaw became the first postmaster for Santa Susanna.

SOUTHERN PACIFIC LOCOMOTIVE, C. 1910. Southern Pacific Engine No. 2068 stops briefly at Moorpark on its way north towards Ventura. The Southern Pacific passenger service allowed residents of Santa Susana to ride north or south to do their business and shopping in one day; it used to take three days for the round-trip by horse and buggy.

CRINKLAW'S STEAM TRACTOR. This massive piece of equipment was the first of its kind in Ventura County. With wheels 7 feet high and 4 feet wide, its towing capacity was unmatched. Shortly after purchase, Crinklaw was contracted to plow a 100-acre field. He hooked thirty-one 10-inch plows behind the Holt Steamer and plowed the field in one day. The rancher felt Crinklaw was making money too fast and refused to pay, but a lawsuit finally brought the rancher to terms.

SANTA SUSANA, 1914. Taken from a vantage point looking north, this photograph shows the early town of Santa Susana. On the south side of Los Angeles Avenue from the left is the Crinklaw home, their garage, the two-story Crinklaw Building, and the Crinklaw store. A young row of eucalyptus trees border Tapo Street and the Wright Ranch. The long dark building at the left is the Southern Pacific warehouse, and the Southern Pacific depot is to the right.

EVA MAHAN CRINKLAW, C. 1900. Eva Mahan Crinklaw is shown driving a spring wagon with her son Harry. When she first saw Simi Valley in 1873, she described it as "a narrow cow trail winding through the valley, sage brush and cactus to the right and left, here and there dotted a sycamore or an elder. Under the trees were herds of cattle and flocks of sheep, seeking refuge from the hot sun."

SANTA SUSANNA DEPOT, 1916. The Southern Pacific Railroad depot is shown blanketed in snow during a rare winter storm in 1916. This unusual Southern California weather occurred the same day as the Santa Susana wedding between Louella Crinklaw and Robert Wright Jr. on December 26, 1916.

PULLMAN CAR, 1906. This photograph of a Pullman car designated "Santa Susana" was recently found but without any accompanying detail. It is possible that this was the railcar used to transport Massachusetts senator George F. Hoar and his family to Simi Valley for a week to visit his nephew Charles Emerson Hoar, who lived at the Humming Bird Nest Ranch in Santa Susana.

OIL GUSHER, TAPO CANYON, C. 1910. One of the first big oil producers is shown in this photograph with the spectators who drove to Tapo Canyon to view the spectacle. In 1900, Robert Shryock drilled the first oil well in Simi Valley, but it was not until 10 years later when the Scarab Oil Company drilled the first wells in Tapo Canyon that it produced significant quantities of oil.

SOUTHERN PACIFIC RAILROAD DEPOT. This view of the railroad depot was taken about 1918 and shows what was termed a "standard 22R depot design." The ticket area was at the west end, the office on the left, and freight platform and storage at the east end. The stationmaster's living quarters were on the second floor. Note the west-facing depot sign, which uses the double-"N" spelling, Santa Susanna.

SOUTHERN PACIFIC WAREHOUSE CREW. This warehouse was built in 1905 by the Southern Pacific Milling Company and was located across the tracks from the train depot. It was used to store hay, grain, beans, nuts, and dried fruit. A fire destroyed the building and 30,000 sacks of beans in 1918 after a drunken employee accidently knocked over the stove.

THE GREAT TUNNEL. Construction crews and equipment are shown at the west portal entrance during construction of "the Great Tunnel." The 7,369-foot tunnel took three and a half years to complete. A dozen or more men were killed during the construction due to cave-ins, asphyxiation, electrocution, and other accidents. The tunnel was completed in July 1904.

RAILROAD SECTION WORKERS. Dan Ralston (left) and an unidentified worker are shown with the one-cylinder "speeder" motor car used to monitor the rails and switches on the Santa Susana section. Dan Ralston later worked in the Tapo Canyon oil fields and was appointed constable of Simi Township after Warren "Sporty" Willard was killed by a burglar in Oxnard.

SANTA SUSANA TUNNEL, 1903. This interior view, taken during the construction of tunnel No. 26, shows the shaft before it was shored with timbers and lined with cement. The work was done by drilling, blasting, and hauling away the debris. Problems with water seepage and lack of air caused numerous delays during the course of its construction.

CONSTRUCTION OF TUNNEL NO. 26. The firm of Erickson and Petterson received the contract to dig the three tunnels through the Santa Susana Mountains to connect the Southern Pacific line through the San Fernando Valley to Los Angeles. The No. 26 tunnel was the longest at 7,369 feet in length; tunnel No. 27 was 824 feet and tunnel No. 28 was the shortest at 537 feet.

SOUTHERN PACIFIC TIMETABLE, 1875. Until completion of the Santa Susana tunnel in 1904, the only way for residents of Simi to get to Los Angeles was to go west. The trains out of Simi Valley went to the Montalvo Junction, then east through Fillmore to the Saugus Junction, and then down the Valley Line through the Newhall tunnel into San Fernando and then to Los Angeles.

SOUTHERN PACIFIC SECTION CAR. The Ralston family used this railroad car for their living quarters while they were working for the railroad. It would remain parked on a siding adjacent to the section they were working and then moved to another spot when needed.

CRINKLAW'S FIRST AUTOMOBILE. The Crinklaw family is shown with their first car, a right-hand-drive Tourist. Horace Crinklaw sits at the steering wheel as his son Harry looks towards the camera. Eva Crinklaw is in the back seat with two of her daughters. The Tourist was produced by a California company in 1905 and featured a four-cylinder engine and seating for five at a cost of about $1,700.

FREIGHT TRAIN AT CHATSWORTH. A Southern Pacific steam engine pulls a long line of freight cars heading towards tunnel No. 28 in Chatsworth. This scene, captured by John Sparhawk Appleton in 1912, was one of two glass plates he exposed that day that formed a two-print panorama showing Stony Point and tunnel No. 29, the third Santa Susana tunnel.

SCARAB OIL WELL, TAPO CANYON. After the wells began producing, the Scarab Oil Company ran a pipeline down the hill to storage tanks near the train depot. The pipeline used gravity flow and can be seen in this photograph at the right side of the picture. Railroad tank cars then loaded the crude oil directly from the storage tanks.

DOHENY PACIFIC PETROLEUM GUSHER. In 1916, Edward Doheny bought 7,500 acres of property from the Patterson Ranch Company in Tapo Canyon along with the oil leases owned by the Petrol Company and the Santa Susana Syndicate. This picture shows one of the wells drilled by the Doheny Pacific Petroleum Company that hit oil on the property the following year.

HARRY CRINKLAW, 1917. This studio portrait of Harry Crinklaw was taken when he was 28 years old. In 1921, he bought a well-drilling outfit, went into the drilling business around Ventura County, and lived most of his life in Simi Valley.

The 1912 CRINKLAW BUILDING. Construction of the Crinklaw Building was made from sandstone quarried in the Susana Knolls and hauled by Horace Crinklaw in his four-horse wagon. The design of the building replicated the floor plan of the North Bangor, Maine, Masonic Hall.

SANTA SUSANA RAILROAD DEPOT. The sign at the east end of the depot used a different spelling from the sign at the west end. The Southern Pacific Company could never explain this dilemma. Note the roof of the Southern Pacific Warehouse behind the platform in this picture dates the photograph to before December 1918 when the building burned to the ground.

SANTA SUSANA OIL WORKERS PICNIC, 1923. Employees of the Pan American Petroleum Company and their families pose for a picture taken at a picnic on the Tapo Rancho in 1923. This panoramic

SANTA SUSANA, 1920s. The sleepy town of Santa Susana is shown looking east across the railroad tracks and the Tapo Street crossing. From left to right are the Southern Pacific depot, the first Crinklaw store, the 1912 Crinklaw building, and the Santa Susana Garage. Note Tapo Street was still a narrow dirt road.

photograph was taken by Keystone of Los Angeles who used a camera with a rotating lens to get the wide view of 4:1 perspective.

SOUTHERN PACIFIC DAYLIGHT EXPRESS. In 1937, the Southern Pacific Company began the morning daylight service between Los Angeles and San Francisco. This real-photo postcard shows the beautiful streamlined GS-4 locomotive that sped through Simi Valley and up the coast. Travel time from Los Angeles to San Francisco was about 10 hours.

SANTA SUSANA SYNDICATE WELLS, C. 1918. This view looking to the hills on the east side of Tapo Canyon shows three of the Santa Susana Syndicate wells. Dan Ralston waits in the car while the photograph is taken. Note the small American flag flying above the radiator that was a popular display at the end of World War I.

BOB CRINKLAW, 1950S. Bob Crinklaw was a third-generation descendant of the Crinklaw family in Simi Valley. He worked on the Tapo oil rigs and pump engines for his father from the time he was a young teenager, but by the 1950s, most of the drilling in Simi Valley was for water wells.

SANTA SUSANA DEPOT, 1974. By the mid-1970s, the Santa Susana depot was showing its age and there were no more agricultural exports. Both the citrus and walnut packinghouses were gone, and the agricultural tracts in Simi Valley had been replaced by single-family homes, strip malls, and business developments.

DEPOT RELOCATION, 1975. This photograph shows the main section of the Santa Susana depot as it was being moved down Los Angeles Avenue on May 9, 1975. The building was relocated to the Susana Knolls, reassembled, and restored at a cost of about $40,000.

SANTA SUSANA RAILROAD DEPOT, 2009. This photograph shows the Southern Pacific depot at its current location, adjacent to the Susana Knolls Park on Katherine Road. The old depot was to be torn down, but efforts by preservationists enabled the Simi Valley Park District to purchase the structure for $1 from the Southern Pacific Company and have it moved.

Three

SANTA SUSANA TOWNSHIP

When the railroad through Simi Valley was complete in 1903, a small business community grew up near the Santa Susana depot. Beginning with the businesses started by the Crinklaw family, other small merchants established roots on the south side of the railroad tracks. Louis Riave, who had the store Whipple and Riave in the Crinklaw Building in 1912, wrote: "The first building across the tracks (north side) was a galvanized affair that housed a blacksmith's shop operated by Mike Kauffman. The first portion of our business across the tracks was built in 1924. I took in the Rosauer brothers as partners, and our firm was Riave and Rosauer Brothers. Ed Rosauer left us in 1926, and the firm changed to Riave and Rosauer. Frank Rosauer withdrew from the firm about 1935 and went into business for himself near the corner of Tapo Street and Cochran. . . . We sold the general store to Mr. Dow, and sold our pharmacy to our druggist. In 1944, the Kerns became the owners of the Santa Susana Hardware, but I stayed until the year 1946, when I resigned the office of Postmaster I had held for 34 years."

The Wright Ranch Estates started in 1958 and marked the first big housing development in Santa Susana. After the homes were built, a large commercial development followed on the west side of Tapo Street that was anchored by the Vons Shopping Bag Market. It opened in 1961 with "Sheriff John" Rovick, a television celebrity, as host to a reported 50,000 shoppers over the first weekend.

Town of Santa Susana. In 1928, Howard Marr of Texas had plans to develop Santa Susana into a model community called Marr-Land. He purchased the 410-acre Crinklaw Ranch, surveyed and laid out lots, built cement sidewalks, and installed electric light poles on the south side of Los Angeles Avenue and Tapo Street. Before he got any further, the Depression hit and all work stopped.

Santa Susana School Class. Rena Crinklaw was the teacher at the Santa Susana School; she is shown standing in the center of the back row in this photograph taken about 1912. Her younger sister, Louella, also taught at the first school, which was located on South Tapo Street and built in 1902.

SANTA SUSANA SCENE, C. 1920. This snapshot shows a film crew shooting the scene of a Western two-reeler in front of the Crinklaw Building. The original merchandise store built 10 years earlier can be seen with an extension added to the front of the building.

SANTA SUSANA SCHOOL. Jerry Haigh remembered, "My teacher, Miss Lou Crinklaw scolded me for riding my saddle horse through the schoolyard at a full gallop. I promised I wouldn't do it anymore, but it was so much fun to see the kids scatter like chickens when they saw me coming. One morning Miss Lou met me at the school barn and had a switch in her hand."

SANTA SUSANA GARAGE AND UNION GAS STATION. This photograph was badly faded but digital technology was used for its restoration. Art McDonald stands between the garage and gas station, and "Sharkey" Ellis and Charlie Green sit on the back of the pickup as two motorists shoot the breeze.

INTERIOR, SANTA SUSANA GARAGE. Bob Barnes and Art McDonald, two veterans who served in World War I, started the Santa Susana Garage about 1919. McDonald works at the bench as his father looks towards the camera. This building was renovated and is still being used today.

Santa Susana Election Precinct, 1918. In 1914, there were 101 registered voters listed in the Santa Susana election precinct—100 more voters than there were a dozen years earlier, in 1902. By 1918, the number dropped to 99, most likely a result of the impact of World War I on the community.

INDEX TO

PRECINCT REGISTER

SANTA SUSANA

Election Precinct

COUNTY OF VENTURA

STATE OF CALIFORNIA

Primary Election, August 27

1918

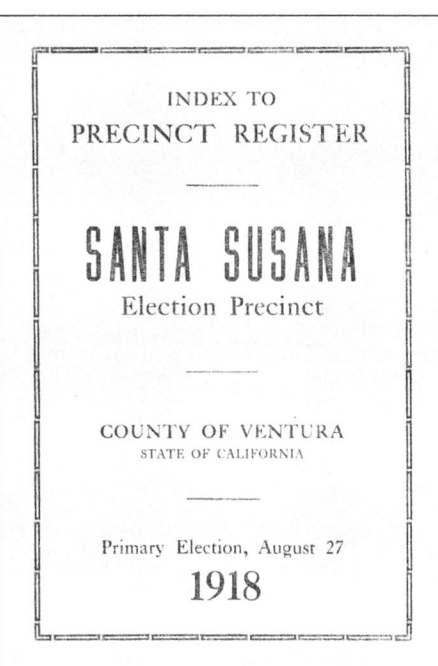

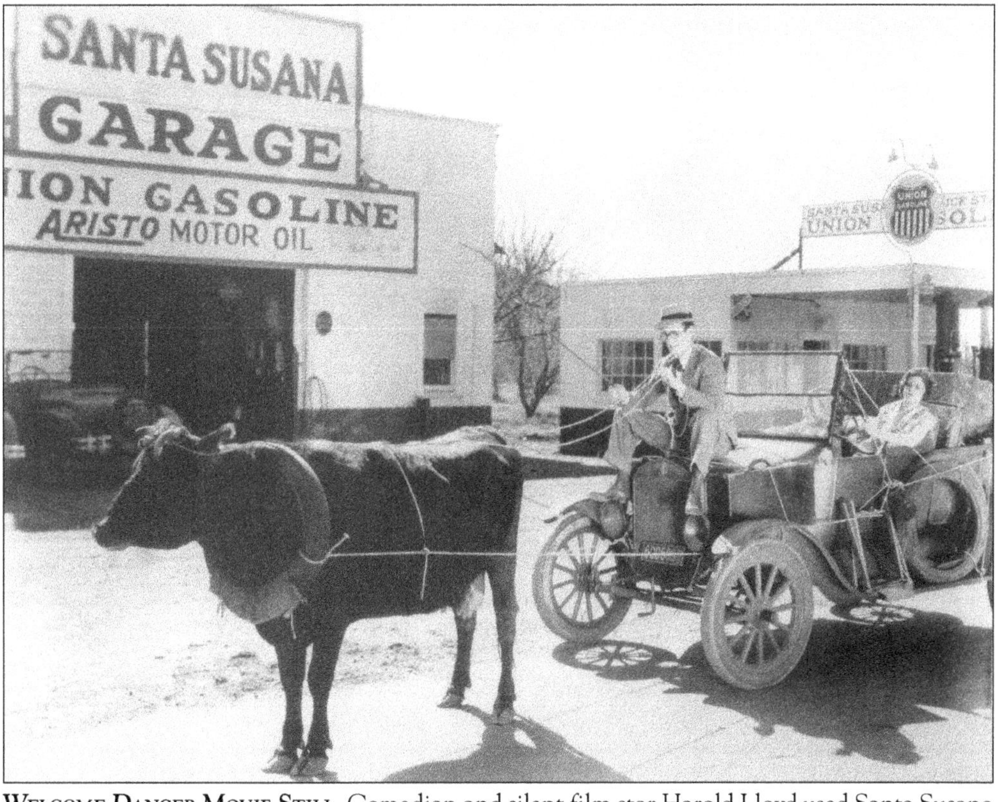

Welcome Danger Movie Still. Comedian and silent-film star Harold Lloyd used Santa Susana as a backdrop for scenes in his 1929 film, *Welcome Danger.* In this sequence, Lloyd and his costar Barbara Kent haul their auto to the Santa Susana Garage because it has run out of gas.

ELK'S CLUB BARBECUE. Brewer Eddie Maier purchased Rancho Potrero del Burro and the Cañada Aliso in 1910. Maier hosted the annual spring outing for Lodge 99 each year, and he invited every Elk Club member in Southern California to his Rancho Special in Santa Susana. Maier was called "one of the greatest of all Elks," by the newspapers.

MAIER BEER LABEL. The Maier Brewing Company of Los Angeles began operating in 1882 and produced over 90 different beer labels during its history. Edward Maier assumed control of the company after his father's death in 1904, and the company continued business until 1971. Brew 102 was born after World War II and was one of their most popular labels.

EDWARD R. MAIER. Brewery king "Eddie" Maier was also owner of the Vernon Baseball Club of the Pacific Coast League. For 20 years, his Santa Susana ranch was the annual site of lavish barbecues that featured baseball games, band concerts, boxing matches, and keg-rolling contests.

SANTA SUSANA SALOON. Located directly across the highway from the railroad depot was Hinkles Place, the only bar that served hard liquor between the San Fernando Valley and Oxnard. The owner, Clark Hinkle, did not drink and was mindful of the sins of alcohol. He had a sign posted above the bar that read, "If your children don't have shoes, don't buy booze."

CLARK HINKLE. Clark Hinkle was born in Illinois, farmed grain in Washington, and raised cotton in Louisiana. Later he migrated west to Texas and started cattle ranching. In the early 1920s, half his herd froze to death on the Texas plains. The next year, the rest of his cattle contracted anthrax and had to be destroyed. Hinkle sold his ranch and came to California.

HINKLES PLACE, INTERIOR. Clark Hinkle (shown at the far end) came to Simi in 1924 from Los Angeles where he was a barber for a short period. He went into the bar business with local veterinarian Dr. Fred Watkins and started Hinkles Place. A card room was located behind the bar, and to the right was a billiard table.

SANDSTORM ACROSS TAPO STREET, 1909. The east wind blew especially hard in Santa Susana, and eucalyptus windbreaks were planted. A January 7, 1924, *Oxnard Daily Courier* news article noted that sand piled up to 6 feet in height against buildings, and "the Crinklaw Garage was almost hidden by a sand dune. The dune was 50 feet in length and the highway two feet deep in places."

SANTA SUSANA GRAMMAR SCHOOL, 1915. The second Santa Susana School was built of bricks and was located on Los Angeles Avenue, one-fourth mile west of Tapo Street. Behind the schoolhouse were a playground and a small home. Three teachers taught classes from first through eighth grades.

RIAVE BUSINESS BLOCK, 1932. Louis Riave and his brother Max built this store on the west side of Tapo Street in 1924. It is one of the few early buildings still doing business in Santa Susana. Located on what was then called First Street, it is now the home of Valley Fair Antiques and Aubergine Emporium on Valley Fair Street.

VELA'S LUNCHEONETTE. Vela Boyer started this small café next door to Santa Susana Hardware in the early 1940s. It served all manner of soda fountain specials, including floats, malts, shakes, and sundaes. Her menu from 1944 showed hamburgers for 30¢ and Coca-Cola for 5¢. Shown are, from left to right, Ida Pierson, Vela Boyer, Peggy McConnell, and Velma Estpiech.

SEASIDE OIL STATION. Herbert "Hub" Litton operated the Seaside Oil Company gas station at the Santa Susana Garage. This photograph from the early 1940s shows Hub on the left waiting on customers Midge and Rusty when a gallon of gas cost just 19¢.

SANTA SUSANA BUSINESSES, 1946. Appleton Radio Service was the first business in Simi Valley to specialize in the sale and repair of radios and phonographs. Next door, Joe Gurican opened the Simi Valley Cleaners, and to the far right of the Crinklaw home, Ellsworth "Skinny" Johnson operated Johnson's Paint and Home Supplies.

LEE HAVINS. One of the first grocery store and meat markets in Santa Susana was started in 1941. Lee Havins purchased the business in 1948, which was then called Roddy's Market, and started Havins Market. This photograph of Havins was taken in front of the bank at Moorpark, the then closest place for business owners from Santa Susana and Simi to do their banking.

DOUGLAS WHITE OAK'S PARK, 1950. Built by Douglas Aircraft Company for employees, White Oak's Park was located at the northeast corner of Simi Valley. By 1949, it had opened to the public. The facility had a large and spacious clubhouse; a skeet-shooting range; baseball diamond; picnic area with badminton, ping-pong, and horseshoe facilities; and this large heated swimming pool with standard- and high-level diving boards.

SIMI VALLEY ADVERTISER. The *Simi Valley Advertiser* was published every Thursday by Earnest Buckner who had a small printing company located on Barnard Street in Santa Susana. The weekly, eight-page publication was distributed by the U.S. Postal Service from 1951 to 1957. Type for the publication was set by hand and printed with a Kelsey Letterpress machine on 9-inch-by-12-inch newsprint paper.

PANTRY CAFÉ, 1958. This small eatery was located just west of Havins Market and was started in 1954 by Lorraine Havins as the Santa Susana Café. A year later, the Woodbury family operated it as the Susana Café, followed by Roy Laney who called it Roy's Café, and by 1958, it was called the Pantry Café. The spot was popular with pilots who flew into the Santa Susana Airport.

APPLETON RADIO AND TELEVISION SERVICE, 1959. By the early 1960s, television sets were in many households and Appleton Radio on Los Angeles Avenue and Tapo Street expanded its business to include sales and service of televisions. The old, two-story Crinklaw home next door now housed two businesses: Dr. L. Lai's dentist office and the office for attorney Gordon Lindeen.

WRIGHT RANCH ESTATES, 1958. This aerial view looking north across Los Angeles Avenue shows the start of the first modern housing development in Santa Susana, the Wright Ranch Estates. The project was built in phases with the Vons Shopping Bag Market commercial section the last phase, which opened for business on December 21, 1961.

Four

Tapo Citrus and Walnut Growers Associations

Two of the most important agricultural commodities produced in Santa Susana were citrus and walnut crops. The Tapo Citrus Association and Simi Valley Walnut Growers Association formed between 1915 and 1920. The associations enabled independent growers of these two crops to maximize their production capabilities. The climate and soil conditions of the Santa Susana District were especially favorable to the growth and production of citrus and walnut trees. The proximity of the citrus and walnut packinghouses to the Southern Pacific Railroad gave growers an added advantage at market time. In the early years of production, the only limitation to the harvest was finding enough available labor, and good paying jobs were available to everyone when it was time to pick the fruit.

The vast production of citrus from the Tapo District was largely a result of the foresight of the Patterson Ranch Company of Oxnard. In 1910, the company began developing small parcels between 5 and 20 acres in the Tapo District. The excellent climate and rich alluvial soil, composed of Yolo silt loam, was considered the best in California. Orchards of Eureka lemons, Valencia oranges, and Washington navels were planted along with Placentia walnuts and Royal apricots. Reservoirs and water systems were established by the Tapo Mutual Water Company, and they supplied each property. The parcels were offered for sale in 1915 just as the young trees were starting to produce fruit. Buyers who were able to take advantage of these citrus and nut ranches saw decades of production with good profitability.

The Tapo Citrus Association had a local packing plant to wash, grade, and pack the oranges to load directly on boxcars. The association provided fertilizer, supplies, and pest control inspections as well as water and soil conservation advice to the growers, and it made sure its members were aware of every method to maximize production. During the Depression years, they brought in the Farmers Production Credit Association that provided loan relief, which was "the greatest thing that ever happened for the farmer," according to citrus rancher Lynford Hess.

The Simi Valley Walnut Growers Association operated similarly to the citrus association. It was a cooperative organization where the farmers banded together to market their produce.

TAPO CITRUS PACKING CREW, 1949. Employees of the Tapo Citrus packing plant pose for a group portrait with samples of the different citrus labels they packed. Walt Frei (center, top row) was the packinghouse foreman.

TAPO CITRUS ASSOCIATION PACKING PLANT, 1950. The Tapo Citrus packing plant was started in 1917 and located at the present-day location of the East County Courthouse near the corner of Tapo Canyon Road and Alamo Street. The railroad ran a 6,815-foot spur to the packinghouse around 1922 to pack crated oranges directly into boxcars. The Tapo plant operated until 1970 when processing was moved to Somis.

Tapo-Brand Citrus Label. In 1925, Tapo-brand Valencia oranges sold at auction on the New York market for $19.15 per box, the highest price ever paid for California oranges. With an average of 176 oranges per box, the price of an individual orange was 15¢.

Women Packing Oranges, 1940s. Workers are shown packing Tapo-brand Valencia oranges in the early 1950s. Shown are, from left to right, Bobbie Schulze, Carmen Magana, Belen Hernandez, Ruth Sepulveda, and Angie Barba.

Joseph Sailer Sr. Joseph Sailer was a founding director of the Tapo Citrus Association and a former mayor of Oxnard. He came to Ventura County to work for the American Beet Sugar Company in 1897. When the company began to develop property in Simi Valley, Sailer purchased a citrus ranch in 1921 and moved his family to the Tapo District.

Humming Bird-Brand Citrus Label. In 1958, Tapo Citrus set a record for Valencia orange production with a harvest of 692,545 field boxes and a yield of 371 boxes per acre. About 1,900 acres of Valencia oranges were under cultivation in the Tapo District of Simi Valley.

NATIVE DAUGHTER CITRUS LABEL. Simi colonist C. G. Austin was the first to plant a grove of citrus in Simi Valley at the corner of Cochran Street and Erringer Road. He grew 1 acre of Washington navels and had moderate success using natural rainfall but realized that good irrigation was the key to successful citrus production.

TAPO CITRUS PACKING CREW, 1937. "Betty" Osborn (far left) heads up a line of packers who boxed oranges at the Tapo Citrus packing plant for Sunkist oranges in the mid-1930s. Behind Osborn are, from left to right, Jessie ?, Erma Griset, Rita Schreiber, Lola ?, Alma Timmons, Etta Ward, Viretta Turner, Minnie Turner, Hattie Hansen, and unidentified.

CALLAHAN RANCH WALNUTS, 1930S. James Callahan and Jim Parnell have large loads of sacked walnuts to go to the walnut house for processing and shipment. During the 1930 season, the Santa Susana District produced 475 tons of walnuts, or about two percent of all Southern California production.

SIMI VALLEY WALNUT HOUSE. The Diamond Walnut House was built in 1929 and covered a ground space of 90 feet by 140 feet alongside the Southern Pacific Railroad tracks. It had two stories, a basement, and cost about $50,000 to build, including the machinery. The Walnut House closed in 1960 after the Camarillo facility became the central processing point.

SIMI VALLEY WALNUT GROWERS ASSOCIATION. The Simi Valley Walnut Growers Association was started in 1915 and continued until the early 1960s. Standardized rates for picking walnuts were set by the state and local grower associations each year. During the harvest season, the Walnut House employed about 30 women and 20 men.

Simi Valley Walnut Growers Association
SIMI, CALIFORNIA

RICHARD BARD, President
O. E. McKENZIE, Vice President
B. H. BRIGHAM, Secretary
CHAS. A. BUSH, Manager

DIAMOND CALIFORNIA WALNUTS

WALNUT PICKING RATES FOR 1943 SEASON

As agreed upon by county wide meeting of growers held at Saticoy, August 10, 1943

All rates based on standard 22 x 36 barley bag level full.

All rates are maximum prices, and for satisfactory completion of season.

COASTAL DISTRICT: Including areas adjacent to Saticoy, Oxnard, Camarillo and Somis.

	Picking clean hulled nuts including shaking from trees	Picking clean hulled nuts without shaking from trees	Picking, no hulling, and including shaking from trees	Picking, no hulling, and without shaking from trees
Budded trees	1.15	.90	.57½	.45
Seedlings	1.35	1.10	.67½	.55

INTERIOR DISTRICT: Including areas adjacent to Moorpark, Simi, Santa Susana, Ojai, Santa Ana, Santa Paula and eastward.

Budded trees	1.25	1.00	.62½	.50
Seedlings	1.45	1.20	.72½	.60

TREE SHAKING LABOR: .75 per hour in all districts.

WALNUT ORCHARD, 1930s. A well-kept walnut orchard stands ready for the picking season at summer's end. Ross Harrington wrote: "You could always tell a walnut picker by looking at his or her hands. If their fingertips were black, you knew that person had picked a lot of nuts." Virginia Barnes added, "We used to see how stained we could get our hands." To some, picking walnuts was a badge of honor. The more picked, the deeper the stains.

ROBERT WRIGHT JR. "Bob" Wright came to Santa Susana from Tennessee with his family in 1910. He helped his father plant 180 acres of walnuts and 20 acres of apricots on the west side of Tapo Street near Cochran Street. He became manager of the Walnut House and was active in many other civic affairs.

SCOTT RANCH WALNUTS, 1950s. Janet (left) and Dougald Cameron (center) are shown with neighbor Phil Davey in front of their harvest of walnuts. Some ranchers preferred to de-hull and dry their nuts before taking them to market. This added more work but paid more and worked well for ranchers with smaller nut crops.

SPRAYING FOR HUSK FLIES, 1940s. The Placentia variety of walnut was the most common nut grown in Simi Valley, but some ranchers also grew Eureka and Payne varieties. Trees were sprayed with a pesticide during the month of May to help control coddling moths and husk flies that caused shriveled and darkened kernels and mold growth.

JOHN ARNOLD APPLETON. Arnold Appleton replaced Bob Wright as manager of the Walnut House and held that position for 15 years until the Walnut House closed in the early 1960s. He was born in Simi Valley in 1898 and witnessed three phases of agricultural transition from dryland barley farming to apricots and plums and finally to citrus and walnuts.

WALNUT POLE SHAKERS. Walnuts were usually harvested while their husks were still green. Long aluminum poles with sturdy hooks were used to shake the branches to knock the nuts to the ground where they would be gathered in buckets. Some ranchers used strong mechanical vibrators that attached to their tractors and could shake the entire tree, significantly speeding up the process.

WALNUTS FROM BERYLWOOD RANCH. From left to right are Mr. Rabey, Mr. Swor, Gus Johnson, and Mr. Allen. The workers are about to take a load of nuts to the Walnut House in Santa Susana. It required about four large buckets of freshly shaken green nuts to fill the burlap bags called gunnysacks. In the 1950s, the average price paid to walnut pickers was $1 per bag, and on a good day, one could fill 20 to 25 sacks.

Five

SANTA SUSANA AIRPORT

Two plane crashes and an emergency landing contributed to the early start of the Santa Susana Airport. In 1937, Simi resident Glenn Fitzgerald flew his plane from Oxnard and landed in a vacant field north of the railroad depot. His Arrow Sport was a low-wing monoplane with an open, side-by-side cockpit and a modified Ford V-8 engine. He walked over to the Santa Susana Garage where Harold Stevens was working and asked if he wanted to go for a ride. The pair took off, and Fitzgerald made a low pass over the garage where spectators were watching. He pulled the plane into a steep climb and bank. The plane lost airspeed, stalled, and crashed into a tomato field halfway between the garage and the creek bed. Twenty-three-year-old Glenn Fitzgerald was killed and passenger Stevens was badly injured but survived. Within a year, the same field where the crash occurred was purchased by Byron "Pop" Dwelle.

Pop owned two planes that he kept at an airport near his Culver City plumbing business. He lived in the Susana Knolls and wanted to be able to fly his plane and land near home. About a year after the Fitzgerald crash, he bought the 20-acre tomato field, graded it with a train rail dragged behind his Model A Ford, and created a landing strip. Later he built a hanger off Tapo Street to protect his planes from the east wind and blowing sand. When World War II started, Dwelle joined the USAF Ferry Command. On one mission, he was ferrying a Lockheed P-38 from Los Angeles to South Carolina when he hit bad weather. During landing, the plane crashed and Pop was killed. After his death, Ellsworth "Gibby" Gibbs operated the landing strip and hanger at Santa Susana. Gibby was dealer for Luscombe Aircraft. He worked out of the hanger for several years until Pop's widow, Gladys Dwelle, decided to sell the property.

"Chet" Foster was a novice pilot flying over Simi Valley when his plane started having engine problems. He spotted the dirt strip at Santa Susana and made an emergency landing, and then hitchhiked back to the Santa Monica Airport to get help. Later during World War II, Foster drove his family out to Santa Susana to show where he had landed. Two years later, he bought the property from Mrs. Dwelle and made improvements, and in 1944, the Santa Susana Airport was officially designated by the FAA.

BYRON "POP" DWELLE. Pop Dwelle graded and leveled out a private landing strip on property running parallel to the Arroyo Simi creek on south Tapo Street that would later become the Santa Susana Airport. Dwelle lived in the Susana Knolls, and before he graded the dirt strip off Tapo Street, he used to land his plane on a field near Katherine Street. He is shown here with his WACO biplane and son Byron "Poose" Dwelle Jr.

SANTA SUSANA LANDING STRIP, C. 1940. This aerial of Santa Susana looking east shows the intersection of Los Angeles Avenue and Tapo Street. The dirt landing strip that used to be planted with tomatoes was graded by Pop Dwelle about 1938. Close inspection shows the airport hanger and only four or five airplanes on the flight line.

SANTA SUSANA AIRPORT, C. 1972. Mel Aldrich took this photograph of the Santa Susana Airport about 1972 at the zenith of its operation, as indicated by the number of aircraft dotting the flight line. Aldrich flew out of Santa Susana and took a number of high-quality aerial photographs of both the airport and the development in Simi Valley during the 1958–1974 period.

MY GAL AT "SANTA SU." This undated photograph of an old Piper Cub and someone's gal posing for a snapshot looks more like a vacant field than an airport. That was the charm of Santa Susana in the early days: a simple dirt landing strip with grassy tie downs, little air traffic, clean air, and beautiful scenic hills.

RYAN PT-22. Henry "Hank" Schaefer flew his PT-22 Ryan Recruit out of Santa Susana for a number of years. Hank was a career officer in the USAF who flew KC135 aerial tankers and retired as a "full bird" colonel. The Ryan plane was built at the beginning of World War II as a trainer; it had a five-cylinder, 160-HP radial engine and was nicknamed the "Maytag Messerschmitt."

C-49. After the war years, pilots started flying the smaller military planes into Santa Susana to test their skills at landing on a small field. No date or information about this plane or photograph is known other than the distinctive hills of Santa Susana that bordered the south side of the airport are in the background.

CRASH IN THE ARROYO SIMI. The aerial photograph on the previous page shows how close one section of the creek comes to the landing strip, and this Piper Cub might have hit a crosswind or simply miscalculated where it touched down and ended up in the creek bed. There is no information about the plane, pilot, or circumstances of this particular crash.

CHESTER FOSTER, 1922. This studio portrait of Chester "Chet" Foster was taken in Los Angeles when he worked in silent pictures. Foster purchased the property that Byron Dwelle had graded and used for a private landing strip in 1943. He and his wife, Lorene, performed all the necessary requirements, and in 1944, the FAA gave the Santa Susana Airport official designation.

WEST END, SANTA SUSANA AIRPORT. This picture from the mid-1950s shows the west end of the airport that bordered the south end of Tapo Street. The Quonset hut next to the hanger served as the pilot's ready room. The Mooney airplane N353A (at the left) made a crash landing after the pilot failed to drop the landing gear, and a group of spectators is seen surveying the wreckage.

DE HAVILLAND GIPSY MOTH, 1956. Shown are, from left to right, unidentified, Joe Pfeifer, and pilot David Watson with his British 1920s-era de Havilland DH-60 at the Santa Susana Airport. The Gipsy Moth was a two-seat biplane of wooden construction, with plywood-covered fuselage and fabric-covered surfaces.

APPROACH TO SANTA SUSANA, 1959. The landing approach to the dirt strip at Santa Susana was tricky. The hill at the east end approach required pilots to either fly a dogleg around the north side or make a direct approach over the hill and set the plane down quickly. The short 1,500-foot strip also had power lines at the west end. This was an added obstacle if a pilot had to abort his touchdown and then regain enough altitude to miss the electrical wires.

PLANE CRASH IN CITRUS GROVE, 1958. Joe Pfeifer (pictured) and Bill Appleton owned this Piper Cub that had to make an emergency landing in a citrus grove near Township Avenue. The pair had just finished fixing and getting the plane airworthy. Appleton went up with an inspection pilot to certify the plane. The inspector turned off the fuel supply, inadvertently thinking it was the carburetor heat. The engine died, forcing a crash landing and the taking out of two trees in John Werner's citrus grove. Both the pilot and the passenger walked away from the crash unhurt.

PLANE OR FLYING BOAT? This homebuilt amphibian was an example of some of the odd-looking experimental planes that came to Santa Susana Airport from time to time. Notice the engine and propeller are not located on the nose of the fuselage but on top of the wing.

"WHIRLYBIRDS" TELEVISION SHOW. Desilu Productions used the Santa Susana Airport in many of their *Whirlybirds* television episodes, where it was cast as the fictitious Longwood Field. The show featured Craig Hill as P. T. Moore and Ken Toby as Chuck Martin and filmed 111 episodes between 1956 and 1960 using a 1953 Bell 47G Helicopter.

SANTA SUSANA AIRPORT, C. 1961. This view looking north over Santa Susana shows the auto wrecking yard and dump that used to be located south of the airport near the creek. Within a few years, the two large walnut orchards surrounding the airport would become housing subdivisions. As Simi Valley increased in population, the Santa Susana Airport began to attract more and more planes, pilots, and students.

WILLIAM H. APPLETON, C. 1956. Bill Appleton had a tie-down and flew out of the Santa Susana Airport for 25 years. His radio and television business was within a block of the runway, and much of his spare time was spent at the airport working on his plane and talking with fellow pilots. His Piper Tri-Pacer N8199C was the very last plane to leave the airport after it was condemned in 1981. He relocated it to the Santa Paula Airport.

CESSNA N11469 NOSES IN. A Cessna 150 flown by a student pilot ends up in the rough off the fairway of the landing strip and suffers major structural damage (note the crack in the fuselage just aft of the rear window). This picture shows the hill one had to fly over (or around) when making a landing. Note the notch cut in the hill where someone tried to decrease its height.

Six

Corriganville Movie Ranch

The Corriganville Movie Ranch was the creation of Ray "Crash" Corrigan, a stuntman and actor in adventure movies and B-Western serials during the 1930s and 1940s. Corrigan was the first Western star to appear on a box of Wheaties, the "Breakfast of Champions" cereal. Corrigan got the idea to invite the public to see how Western pictures were made. He opened the gates of his ranch in 1949, and it became an immediate success, attracting thousands of people. By 1953, Corriganville was rated among the top 10 most interesting places in America.

For fun and entertainment, Corriganville offered endless choices for the whole family. In the morning, one could have breakfast with Crash Corrigan and his friends at the Last Frontier Café where there was a chance to meet Western movie and television stars like Nick Adams of *The Rebel* or Peter Brown of *Lawman*, or the *Lone Ranger* and Tonto. On the streets of Silvertown, one could watch reenactments of the *Killing of Billy the Kid*, a bank robbery, or *Gunfight at the O.K. Corral*. On the outskirts of town, there were rides on a Wells Fargo stagecoach, or one could take a train ride on a scale model of an 1863 Southern Pacific steam engine. Or one could simply ride horseback around the ranch.

From Silvertown it was a short walk to Fort Apache. This set was used for the John Ford movie of the same name and later for the *Rin-Tin-Tin* television series. From there, one could go to the rodeo arena and watch bronco riders, trick ropers, and rodeo clowns. After the rodeo, one could take a shuttle back to Silvertown, drink real draft beer at the Silver Dollar Saloon, and watch dance hall girls do the cancan or visit the Corriganville Trading Post for leather goods and souvenirs. Then it was off to the shooting gallery to try a fast-draw contest, and then one could walk back to Sherwood Forest and Robin Hood Lake, locations that were used for filming *Jungle Jim* and *Bomba, the Jungle Boy* television series.

ENTRANCE TO CORRIGANVILLE. Corriganville was the "Home of Western Stars and Home of Western Pictures." The entrance, located on Highway 118, opened on May 1953 and was located just north of the Susana Knolls area on present-day Kuehner Drive. The main entrance to Corriganville was hard to miss, and on weekends, the actors and stunt people would often line the roadside dressed as cowboys and American Indians to greet arriving motorists.

"THROUGH THESE GATES PASS THE WORLD'S MOST FAMOUS PEOPLE." This publicity photograph shows actress Elaine DuPont receiving the keys to a new Pontiac from an unidentified car salesman as Crash Corrigan looks on. The distinctive sign under which visitors would pass as they drove in to park was a Corriganville trademark. Corrigan and DuPont were married in 1956 after Corrigan was divorced from his first wife, Rita Jane.

RAY "CRASH" CORRIGAN. This publicity still shows Ray "Crash" Corrigan during the period of 1936–1943 when he was making the very popular *Three Mesquiteers* series for Republic Studios. Crash was born February 14, 1902, in Milwaukee, Wisconsin, and was the second child of Bernhard and Ida Benitz. His given name, Raymond Benitz, was later changed to Bernard, then Benard. It was during his time with Republic Studios that he was given the surname Corrigan.

BANK ROBBERY IN PROCESS. Visitors to Corriganville saw a variety of stunt shows that were often reenactments of historical events. Some of the more popular were *Gunfight at the O.K. Corral*, the *Shooting of Belle Starr*, the *Killing of Billy the Kid*, and the *Hanging of Cattle Kate*. There were about 40 scripted stunt shows designed to showcase the versatility of the Corriganville stuntmen in gun fights, saloon brawls, bank robberies, stage holdups, and street shoot-outs.

CRASH CORRIGAN AND SULTAN. This and several other color postcards were used to promote Corriganville in the 1950s as well as a series of black-and-white postcards picturing the key features of the movie ranch. The reverse side text of this card reads, "Crash Corrigan and Sultan at Corriganville from the Range Buster Series, ready to greet you and show you how and where Western movies are made. 29 miles northeast of Hollywood near Chatsworth."

FORT APACHE SET. John Ford built the Fort Apache set on Table Mountain in Corriganville for his 1948 film *Fort Apache*, starring John Wayne and Henry Fonda. The fort was a replica of a post–Civil War Western outpost and was later used for the main setting of the television series *The Adventures of Rin-Tin-Tin* that ran from 1954 to 1959.

WELCOME TO SILVERTOWN. Crash Corrigan and his horse Flash are shown on the main street of Silvertown in this publicity still welcoming visitors to Corriganville. Corrigan was a tireless promoter and spent considerable time publicizing his Western theme park to the public. He relished his role as host and was always available to have his picture taken with visitors and sign autographs for his fans.

CRASH AND A GROUP OF FANS. Corrigan's Western movie ranch attracted visitors from all over Southern California and from points beyond. They came as individuals, families, school classes, and larger groups. Crash was always available to welcome them, sign autographs, take pictures, let them sit on his horse, and even handle his six-shooters.

AL JENNINGS, ELAINE DUPONT, AND BUD BRESH. Corriganville hosted appearances by many Western film actors and celebrities over the years. Al Jennings (left) was a real Western figure who had been an Oklahoma attorney in the 1890s and later turned to robbing banks and stores after his brother was killed. He later acted in silent films and poses here with actress Elaine DuPont and Corriganville photographer Bud Bresh during his visit to the movie ranch.

SILVERTOWN, EAST END. This view looking south shows the east end of Silvertown taken from a hill adjacent to the Fort Apache set. The Santa Susana Pass road can be seen on the hill at the top of the photograph. At the left is the barn where horses for hire were boarded, and across the street was the two-story stage and dance hall.

ROY ROGERS. Roy Rogers was another popular actor who filmed many Western television episodes and movies at the Corriganville Movie Ranch. One was *Susanna Pass*, the 1949 Republic Studios production starring Rogers, Dale Evans, and Roy's horse, Trigger. The name of the film was obviously taken from the road adjacent to Corriganville, but the plot line had to do with bad guys wanting to dynamite a fish hatchery, so they can get at oil deposits that lay underneath the lake.

SILVERTOWN, WEST END. This photograph shows the west end of Silvertown and is a continuation of the picture on page 152. At the far right behind the large oak tree is Crash Corrigan's house, formerly the old Scott Ranch homestead. To the left of the picture is the back of the two-story structure used as the Silver Dollar Saloon and dance hall.

RODEO BRONCO RIDER. A bronco rider tries to stay in the saddle for the eight-second count at one of the many rodeos sponsored by Corriganville. The rodeo shows were run by Bob Ward in the early years and later by Dee Cooper. In 1953, KNBC Channel 4 began broadcasting a one-hour live show called *Rodeo Roundup* that aired on Saturday afternoons. The rodeos were popular, as can be seen by the number of spectators lining the arena.

CORRIGANVILLE OSTRICH RACE, 1956. Chief Thundercloud provided a rare bit of entertainment to spectators at the Corriganville Rodeo during the ostrich race. Thundercloud was a Cherokee Indian whose real name was Victor Daniels, and he was the original Tonto of the *Lone Ranger* television series. He was a regular celebrity who appeared at Corriganville for a number of years until his death in 1955.

LARRY PARSON, PHOTOGRAPHER. Larry Parson was the younger of the two official Corriganville photographers, Bresh and Parson, and is shown riding Crash Corrigan's horse Flash. Parson started shooting pictures at the Corriganville Movie Ranch in 1953 and worked until about 1960. His collection of original negatives numbers about 4,000 and is one of the best existing collections of images showing the history of the movie ranch.

CORRIGANVILLE RODEO CREW. Larry Parson photographed this group of Corriganville Rodeo performers during one of the shows during the mid-1950s. The rodeo shows featured some of the best bronco and bull riders in the area. The rodeo area seated almost 4,000 people and featured a number of Western shows and riding contests.

SHOW AT ROBIN HOOD LAKE. Spectators line the edge of Robin Hood Lake for a stunt show under a canopy of native oak trees in Sherwood Forest. The lake was used as a film location for the television series *Jungle Jim, Ramar of the Jungle,* and *Bomba, the Jungle Boy.* Corrigan built an underwater camera port at one end of the lake, which gave production companies the ability to film underwater sequences such as Jungle Jim wrestling with a giant African crocodile.

CORSICAN VILLAGE. The Corsican Village set was constructed for the Howard Hughes film production of *Vendetta*, starring Faith Domergue in 1950. It was located south of the Fort Apache set at the base of rocky hill, which overlooked Silvertown. This set was built to resemble the village of Pietranera in 1825 French-controlled Corsica. The set remained as a place for the public to explore and gradually fell to a state of ruin in the late 1950s.

VENTURA COUNTY DEPUTY SHERIFFS. Five deputies from the Ventura County sheriff's office pose for photographer Larry Parson in front of the sheriff's office in Silvertown. Some Ventura County deputies worked at the Corriganville Movie Ranch on weekends doing private security work while others worked larger events in an official capacity doing crowd control.

ROBIN HOOD LAKE. The small creek that flows from the base of the Santa Susana Mountains at the back of the movie ranch and down into Simi Valley is the beginning of the Arroyo Simi. Corrigan initially dammed up the creek bed to construct a pond and later had it paved to preserve water loss. He named it Robin Hood Lake, as it bordered the Sherwood Forest area of the ranch. Stunt shows were staged from the rock at the left of the picture where the two riders appear.

TOURISTS IN SILVERTOWN. In between the stunt shows and movie-making demonstrations, tourists were allowed to wander around the main street and explore the movie ranch. There were concession stands, shops, musical entertainment, a shooting gallery, and the Frontier Railway where one could ride a scale model of the C. P. Huntington steam engine around the perimeter of Silvertown.

COWGIRLS AT CORRIGANVILLE. A group of attractive cowgirls pose for the camera in front of the Silvertown sheriff's office. Besides the appearance of the movie and television actresses, the movie ranch held photo shoots, both public and private, where print models and bathing beauties were available for amateur photographers and shutterbugs.

Seven
SUSANA KNOLLS AND SANTA SUSANA FIELD LABORATORY

Before it was officially designated the Susana Knolls, the area at the foot of the Santa Susana Pass was called Green Haven, Mortimer Park, and to some, Poverty Gulch. The Mortimer Park name was most widely recognized. About 1924, Louis Mortimer and his wife were returning to Los Angeles and had to take a detour through the Simi Valley because of construction on the Conejo Grade. They had never been in the area before and were immediately taken with the beauty of the hills with studded oaks and rocky outcroppings. They purchased the 1,787-acre tract that included the Knolls and divided it into 18 tracts. What ensued were numerous irregular lots, inadequate roads, and overlapping survey lines that have plagued homeowners ever since. In 1944, the ladies of the Knolls Garden Club named the streets and petitioned the county to change the name of the community. They felt Mortimer had slighted the residents with his lack of community development. Nonetheless, by 1955, the Susana Knolls had a county fire station, two churches, a home for the aged, several cafés, a grocery store, and a post office. There was also a blacksmith shop, a realty office, Corriganville, a veterinarian, a large turkey ranch, and the Susana Knolls County Park.

The Santa Susana Field Laboratory (SSFL), built by North American Aviation in 1949, was called the "Hill." There were a number of sites used for testing rocket engines by the Rocketdyne division as well as the Atomics International division. At one time, there were as many as 6,000 employees working around the clock, many who lived in Simi and Santa Susana. To get to work from Simi Valley, one had to drive through the Knolls and up Black Canyon Road to get to the Hill. Longtime SSFL engineer John McCarthy aptly wrote, "When the ground shakes and roaring thunder flaps your pants and pounds your chest, when brilliant lights flare the sky and a towering cloud batters into the high heavens, only in Simi do people smile and have happy faces."

SANTA SUSANA HILLS PROSPECTUS, 1920s. This illustration by the Southern California Investors Corporation of Los Angeles shows an idyllic setting where the development company has planned a community bathing pool with clear mountain spring water. The brochure promises "there are no poisonous insects at Santa Susana Hills and the steep, high peaks will tax the stamina of the most experienced nimrod." The initial lots were 30 feet by 50 feet and started at $100.

LILES GROCERY STORE. Charles and Mabel Liles came to Mortimer Park in the mid-1930s and started this small store at the corner of Oak Knolls Road and Katherine Street. They continued until the end of World War II when Pat Connelly took over the business. In 1952, Opal and Ed Calligan purchased the store and operated it for 18 years until it was sold to the Perez family.

SANTA SUSANA PASS ROAD, 1920s. Looking east up the Santa Susana Pass, this photograph shows the roadway before it was paved with asphalt. This route over the pass was the third road built and opened in 1915. The small building at the left was a real estate office used for property sales in Mortimer Park, and across the road was the vineyard owned by Joe Smith.

SUSANA KNOLLS CHURCH, 1945. Rev. Thomas Grice was the pastor of the Susana Knolls congregation that began during the start of World War II. Knolls Church, shown in this 1945 picture, was used into the mid-1960s then moved and converted to a private residence.

SANTA SUSANA PASS, 1910. The second route over the Santa Susana Pass was built in 1895 to replace the old Coast Stage route. It followed a more gradual ascent around the hill at the west portal of the railroad tunnel. This photograph shows the road in the early days of the automobile. Because it was originally built for horse and wagon, this route was replaced five years later with the current road, which was better suited for automobiles.

PASS CLUB BUSINESS CARD. Located on a hill half the way up the Santa Susana Pass adjacent to the Box Canyon turnoff, the Pass Club was a restaurant and card club run by Margaret "Millie" Coons. The restaurant featured good food and had a great view of Simi Valley. It was known for its card room where one could play Pan and Lo-Ball poker with low-limit betting.

JOEL MCCREA AND MERLE HOLLIS. Actor Joel McCrea and Ventura County sheriff deputy Merle Hollis are shown at a 1950s fund-raising event. Deputy Hollis patrolled all the area east of Moorpark, including Susana Knolls and Box Canyon. In 1953, Hollis captured fugitive Walter Byrd who murdered his estranged wife at her home in Susana Knolls. Hollis tracked Byrd to an abandoned shack at the back of Corriganville and took him into custody without incident. Byrd was executed at the San Quentin gas chamber in 1955.

MORTIMER PARK, 1930s. The development of Mortimer Park was originally intended for small cabins and weekend retreats, but by the end of the 1930s, there were a number of full-time residents. Thelma Riess, an active member of the Knolls Garden Club, petitioned the county in 1944 to have the name Mortimer Park stricken and replaced with Susana Knolls. Her petition claimed that the Mortimer name was not worthy of the distinction due to the lack of community development and poor planning.

COCA CLASSIC, 1975. Located in Area II, the COCA area was used to test the Space Shuttle Main Engines (SSME). The property was owned by North American Aviation until 1958 when it was deeded to the U.S. Air Force. In 1973, the property, including the test facility, was transferred to NASA for the Space Shuttle program. This evening silhouette shows one of the two assemblies used to test SSMEs for the space shuttle program.

BURRO FLATS, 1946. This movie still, taken during the production of the 1946 Ray Milland film, *California*, shows the area the Spanish named *Putrero del Burro*. Burro Flats was a popular place used by early Simi residents for picnics. The location was selected in 1949 by James "Dutch" Kindelberger and Lee Atwood of North American Aviation for the Santa Susana Field Laboratory.

BOWL AREA, FIRST ENGINE HOT FIRE, 1950. The first full-thrust, pump-fed, engine hot fire took place in 1950. This photograph shows that initial test on Vertical Test Stand I, a copy of the World War II test facility at Peenemunde on the Baltic Coast where the Germans developed the V-2 rocket. VTS I was designed to hold not just the engine but also the entire rocket.

NORTH AMERICAN AVIATION EXECUTIVE OFFICERS. North American Aviation moved to Southern California in 1948 and began building their testing facility for liquid-fueled rockets in the Santa Susana Mountains overlooking Simi Valley. Shown are, from left to right, NAA president Lee Attwood, Ray Price, Andy Lambeth, Stan Smithson, and CEO James "Dutch" Kindelberger.

VTS II, 1954. North American Aviation's Santa Susana Field Laboratory modified its engine test stands to accommodate each new rocket engine. This internal company photograph shows the next generation engine test stand, designed to support and test just the engine assembly.

AREA II TEST STANDS. The three Alpha Area test stands were activated in 1955 to support the testing of the Navaho, Atlas, Thor, and Jupiter programs. This photograph shows workers inspecting the facilities after a rare snowstorm on January 30, 1957.

MAIN ENGINE, SPACE SHUTTLE. Jake Hayes makes an adjustment to a Space Shuttle Main Engine (SSME), made by Pratt and Whitney, in this photograph from 1979. The space shuttle was powered by three SSMEs that burned liquid hydrogen and oxygen. The engines provided 490,850 pounds of thrust and collectively consumed 1,035 gallons of propellant per second.

THREE ENGINE FIRING, BOWL AREA. In 1954, German rocket physicist and engineer Werner von Braun was invited to visit the testing facilities at the Santa Susana Field Laboratory. To commemorate his visit, Rocketdyne simultaneously fired three rocket engines, a test that had never been performed before. Above is a picture of that test firing conducted on March 28, 1954.

VERTICAL TEST STAND 3B. Located in the Bowl Area, VTS 3B was activated in 1955 and supported the Navaho, Redstone, Thor, Jupiter, Atlas, and Saturn-V programs. The truck and worker on the flame pit in the foreground give a good idea of the size of this test stand.

ROCKETDYNE MACHINE SHOP. Members of the machine shop at Rocketdyne pose for a group photograph with the various tools of their trade. There are the only three individuals identified in this photograph from the mid-1950: shop foreman Jack Danielson (kneeling, far left), Neil Havens (kneeling, far right), and John Werner (standing, second from right).

Eight

GRANDMA PRISBREY'S BOTTLE VILLAGE

Bottle Village is located in the old Kadota Fig section of Santa Susana on Cochran Street, once home to orchards, pigeon farms, and chicken ranches. Today it is wedged between a condominium complex on one side and an RV storage facility on the other. The 40-foot frontage is so small that most people do not even notice it when they drive by.

When Tressa "Grandma" Prisbrey and her husband, Albert, bought the Santa Susana property in 1956, they never envisioned what would transpire. "Four years ago when we bought this third acre of hilly Santa Susana soil," she recalled. "We leveled it off and moved our trailer onto it. My husband, who had always been a construction worker, got a job at Rocketdyne, and I took the wheels off the trailer. I made pretty sure that we weren't going to do any more meandering about the country, if I could do anything to prevent it, and trailers don't get along well without wheels. I hid the wheels, so we had to stay put." The trailer was a 1946 Royal Spartanette, and Grandma was now 60 years old.

With the wheels off the trailer, Grandma spent the first year at her new home babysitting her grandchildren. She had seven children from her first marriage, but it was time for something new. She began construction on her first bottle house in 1957 as a place to store her pencil collection. When that was done she needed another place for a doll collection, and within a span of four years, she had created an entire village of folk art assemblies. There were 16 freestanding structures made mostly of recycled bottles that were gathered from the local dump. The structures were interlaced with mosaic walkways of cement, impressed with thousands of found objects ranging from buttons, license plates, tile fragments, bottle caps, keys, toy guns, scissors, padlocks, marbles, horseshoes, radiator caps, bullet casings, and anything else that was relatively flat and that could lend itself to a decorative touch. "Everyday for nearly four years, I have gone to the dump unless I happen to be in town," she said. "I spend a lot of time picking over stuff. I drive a Studebaker truck, so I have lots of room to put junk in."

Today Bottle Village is a California State Historical Landmark on the National Register of Historic Places and a Ventura County Cultural Landmark.

TRESSA LUELLA PRISBREY (1896–1988). Tressa "Grandma" Prisbrey built the majority of Bottle Village over a period of four years. It was an amazing feat considering she was over 60 years old and used mostly found materials that she hauled from the dump on south Tapo Street. Add to the equation tons of hand-mixed mortar and more than two million used bottles, and her feat almost seems impossible for one individual to accomplish. (Photograph by Thomas Lane.)

GRANDMA'S DOLLHOUSE. This structure housed Tressa's doll collection, which once numbered over 600 dolls. It was built of blue Milk of Magnesia bottles set with white cement. The front of the structure was shaped to resemble the two rounded curves of a heart. Notice the interplay of bottle walls facing both in and out on either side of the windows.

TRESSA EXPLAINS BOTTLE VILLAGE. Grandma enjoyed interacting with people and usually gave visitors a guided tour around her village of whimsical structures, mosaic walkways, and cactus gardens. "I am a cook's tour, all by myself," she wrote, "because a lot of people won't go around by themselves unless I go along, and tell them about things." (Photograph by Thomas Lane, c. 1969.)

CLEOPATRA'S BEDROOM, 2008. A recent visitor to Bottle Village walks down the mosaic walkway between the TV Tube Wall and Cleopatra's Bedroom during an open house on November 23, 2008. This structure is one of eight that survived the 1994 quake in fairly good condition, owing to the fact that its internal structural support comes from four telephone poles.

EXTERIOR DETAIL. Grandma suspended a total of 1,200 bottles from the eucalyptus trees on the east side of her property to act as wind chimes. In her Rumpus Room, 200 painted gourds hung from the ceiling. This detail shows Grandma's use of pinecones to decorate the exterior of her structures.

GRANDMA AND SHRINE TO ALL FAITHS, 1974. "Crossing over the midway of my place, and turning the corner of the bottle house itself, is my Shrine to all faiths," wrote Grandma. "Since people of every belief visit my Bottle Village, I wanted to have a representation of the major religions." Six hundred blue Milk of Magnesia bottles cover the base of the shrine. (Photograph by Seymour Rosen.)

WISHING WELL, 1960s. This multitiered circular structure was made from blue Milk of Magnesia bottles on the bottom tier, automobile headlights on the second level, and more Milk of Magnesia bottles on the third level with a wooden-roof structure supported by two beams. The Wishing Well was destroyed by the Northridge earthquake.

ROUND HOUSE INTERIOR. This detailed photograph was taken in the Round House, a circular structure that is constructed 3 feet below ground level. "The half circle counter was first intended to be a selling place," Grandma said. "But that idea died before it was born because I don't have time to sell things. It's made of flat pint whiskey bottles." The Round House holds all things round.

PORTRAIT WALL AND LEANING TOWER OF BOTTLE VILLAGE, 1977. The Leaning Tower of Bottle Village uses a decorated beer keg as its base. Behind the tower is the portrait wall, made of various bottles and decorated with small round portraits of Grandma Prisbrey's children and family. (Photograph by Linda Lorr.)

THREE-SIDED STRUCTURE, 1969. This structure sat at the front of the property facing east, and the bottle wall behind it enclosed one of the two trailers on the property. The roof is decorated with broken glass of many colors, and the support posts are trimmed with tin can lids. This structure was lost during the 1994 earthquake. (Photograph by Cherie Raciti.)

GRANDMA AND DOLLHOUSE, 1969. "We have a dump here, in Santa Susana, where everything under the sun shows up if you wait long enough," said Grandma. "It's a graveyard for lost articles, discarded treasures, worn out everything. Especially dolls—I found so many dolls I couldn't resist the temptation to bring them home and dress them." (Photograph by Cherie Raciti.)

PENCIL COLLECTION. Grandma Prisbrey built three different structures to house her pencil collection, estimated at 17,000 pencils. This detail, taken before the 1994 earthquake that heavily damaged most of her displays, shows some of the various pencil mosaics she constructed to display her collection.

GRANDMA PRISBREY REFLECTS. "There was a man here one day," said Grandma, "and he said, 'Lady, this place is going to make you famous some day.' Yes, maybe after I'm dead, I thought. Which reminds me, there was a little hunchbacked lady here one day who was ninety-three years young! Isn't it wonderful when you can keep your wits at that age and still be able to get around." (Photograph by Bob Dawson.)

AFTER THE 1994 EARTHQUAKE. The damage wrought on Bottle Village by the Northridge earthquake of January 17, 1994, destroyed 9 of the 16 freestanding structures and severely damaged the structural integrity of those that did not crumble to the ground. As a result of the quake, Bottle Village remains in a state of arrested decline, but its dedicated group of supporters refuse to allow its demise.

Nine

COMMUNES, CULTS, AND THE WKFL

Three enigmatic religious groups were drawn to the secluded hills surrounding Santa Susana in the 20th century and established communes. Their charismatic leaders dreamed of creating an ideal state or righting the wrongs of society, but those who used self-formulated creeds to attract followers may have had hidden plans.

The earliest of these groups was Pisgah Grande, established in 1914 by Dr. Finis E. Yoakum as a Pentecostal Christian community. It was located 7 miles northeast of Santa Susana in Las Llajas Canyon. Dr. Yoakum and his converts constructed a small town on 3,200 acres that was completely self-sustaining. The Pisgah movement was "devoted to the material welfare, bodily healing, moral uplift, and spiritual life of the stricken in body, victim of drink, outcast, cripple, hungry, friendless, and whosoever is in need of the waters of life." At its zenith, the Pisgah Grande colony had some 30 buildings and 150 full-time residents but ended in 1920 with the death of Dr. Yoakum.

In 1924, Rev. May Otis Blackburn began a religious commune in the high reaches of the Susana Knolls. The Blackburn cult was named The Divine Order of the Royal Arms of the Great Eleven, and it used the hope of immortality to exploit unfortunates seeking spiritual guidance. Some called it the Sixth Seal cult because Blackburn was writing a book titled *The Great Sixth Seal*. She claimed her book would reveal the mysteries of the universe as given to her by God through the Archangel Gabriel. Mother May and daughter Ruth Weiland were simply flapper-era grifters. The bizarre and nefarious acts of the Great Eleven Club came to light in 1929 when May and Ruth were convicted of grand theft in Los Angeles.

In 1949, self-styled messiah Krishna Venta established the WKFL Fountain of the World commune in Box Canyon off the Santa Susana Pass. The wisdom, knowledge, faith, and love commune had a mission to gather the 144,000 elect before the world erupted into a global war. Krishna was assassinated on December 10, 1958, by two disgruntled ex-members who exploded 20 sticks of dynamite, killing themselves, Venta, and seven other commune members.

APPROACH TO PISGAH GRANDE. Pisgah Grande was located about 7 miles northeast of the town of Santa Susana in Las Llajas Canyon. This photograph shows the approach up the canyon and the Pisgah prayer tower on the hill (in the distance). Numerous brick and wooden structures were located at the base of the canyon to the left of the prayer tower and at one time included 150 converts who lived in a self-sustained communal existence.

LECTURE HALL AND YOAKUM RESIDENCE. This view shows the two-story brick lecture/dining hall and adjoining kitchen plus the small residence used by Dr. Yoakum when he stayed at Pisgah Grande. These buildings marked the entrance to the commune with other buildings scattered on either side of the road and stream that followed the base of the canyon. The prayer tower was located on the hill behind the point where this picture was taken.

Dr. Yoakum's "Healing By the Lord." This small 50-page pamphlet was Dr. Yoakum's testimony, and he recounted the accident in Colorado that almost took his life. After his miraculous recovery, he vowed forever to do the Lord's work. Within the pamphlet, he states, "May these unvarnished narratives lead some other afflicted ones to come to the Great Healer, and know what it means where it is written, 'Jesus Christ maketh thee whole.'" In Los Angeles, Dr. Yoakum walked the back alleys among the down-and-outs and social outcasts, calling to give themselves to Christ. He was known to pass out nickels, which just paid for the Red Line fare to his Pisgah Home in Highland Park.

Pisgah Grande Watchtower. The two-story Pisgah Watchtower was constructed of bricks made and fired by workers at the commune. This structure was used as a communal prayer tower and had windows on both floors facing in all four directions where a never-ending vigil was kept by members who prayed in shifts, 24 hours a day.

DR. FINIS EWING YOAKUM (1851–1920). "Daddy Yoakum," as he was called by many of his converts, was dedicated to the teachings of the Lord and was a charismatic leader who championed the idea of providing services for those less fortunate. Besides Pisgah Grande, he founded in and around Los Angeles the Pisgah Home for Nameless Children, the Pisgah Free Store, the Pisgah Ark for rescued girls and women, the Pisgah Gardens, and the Pisgah Home in Highland Park.

YOAKUM FAMILY, HIGHLAND PARK. Dr. FEY (seated in center), as he is called by his family today, is shown at his home in Highland Park with his wife, Mary; twin daughters, Ruth and Ruby (top right); and sons, Finis E. Jr. (left front), Charles (top center), and Modrall (right front). When Dr. Yoakum died in August 1920, so did the Pisgah movement leadership. Within a few months, the residents of Pisgah Grande began to gradually move away until the last holdouts were evicted by the County of Los Angeles.

May Otis Blackburn and Ruth Weiland, 1929. May Otis Blackburn (left) and her daughter Ruth Wieland (right), photographed at the start of their trial for grand theft, were the brains and beauty behind the nefarious acts of the Sixth Seal cult. "Queen Ruth," as she was called, had been married several times, was a one-time taxi dancer, and was known to be a "girl of many loves." May Otis Blackburn was married to Ward Blackburn, a man 26 years younger than she and the son of her mother's husband. The plaintiff at the trial was wealthy Beverly Hills oilman Clifford Dabney who alleged that May and Ruth had swindled him out of $10,000 to help finance the writing of her book, *The Great Sixth Seal*.

Los Angeles Headlines, 1929. This collage of Los Angeles newspaper clippings written during the Blackburn trial illustrates some of the bizarre stories associated with May Otis and her cult, The Divine Order of the Royal Arms of the Great Eleven. The cult headquarters was located in a crescent-shaped temple in the Susana Knolls at the top of Crown Hill Road. The cult compound was the scene of strange activities, including midnight animal sacrifices, unorthodox medical experiments, nude dances, chanting, and missing person reports. Reports claimed the cult began in 1919 in Oregon and moved to Southern California in 1925.

GABRIEL'S TRUMPET. Much of the Blackburn cult dogma was based on information given directly to May Otis Blackburn by St. Gabriel. May claimed she spoke with God through the archangel and would go into a trance to receive his directives. Her literary masterpiece, *The Great Sixth Seal*, would reveal mysteries of the universe and the locations of gold, oil, and other mineral deposits. A previous publication, *The Seventh Trumpet of Saint Gabriel*, was printed in seven editions to "concord with the seven tones of Gabriel's Trumpet."

GRAVE OF REVEREND BLACKBURN (1876–1951). The final resting place of May Otis Blackburn is at Valhalla Memorial Park in North Hollywood, next to the plots of her mother, Jeanne, and her husband, Walter Blackburn. May led her followers from the heights of the sublime to the depths of the ridiculous. One writer of the time said of the cult, "Its ceremonials savored of the rituals practiced by the Black Magicians of the Middle Ages."

FRANCIS HIENDSWATZER PENCOVIC. Prior to formation of the WKFL Fountain of the World, Krishna used his real name, Dr. Francis Hiendswatzer Pencovic. He alleged he was born in Russia and had graduated from the University of Virginia with a medical degree. Later he appeared at lectures behind a drape of fabric as a shadow known only as "the Voice." In another phase, he wore a turban and claimed he was a mystic seer. "What am I?" Krishna once said in answer to a question from a reporter. "I am what I am today, with nothing of what I was yesterday." In 1948, Krishna appeared in the annual Passion play at the Pilgrimage Theatre in Hollywood. For the part, he let his hair grow long and wore a Biblical robe. When the production ends, Krishna vows to continue wearing the robe and letting his hair and beard grow long and walk barefoot until peace comes to the Earth.

FOUNTAIN OF THE WORLD COMMUNE, C. 1949. This shows an early group of the Fountain of the World commune when they lived at the Chatsworth Lake Lodge property. Krishna Venta is not pictured and was probably on the lecture circuit at the time. Note that only two of the members had made the transition to wearing robes. At the left with the beard was Brother Paul (Martin Baker), and at the far right was Brother Elzibah (Peter Kamenoff). Both were killed in the 1958 bombing when Kamenoff and another exploded 20 sticks of dynamite.

KRISHNA IS RELEASED FROM JAIL, 1955. This photograph was taken just after Krishna was released from a five-day stint at the Oakland jail for failure to pay his ex-wife's child support. Krishna argued that as head of the Fountain of the World commune he had no income and that a religious leader should not be subject to pay child support. His case went to the California Supreme Court and is part of divorce case law. In *Pencovic v. Pencovic*, the court ruled that a parent cannot evade support obligations by claiming a religious exemption.

DECEMBER 10, 1958, EXTRA. This final night edition of the *Los Angeles Evening Herald Express* illustrates the tabloid nature that immediately enveloped the WKFL bombing story. News of the disaster took on epic proportions in all of the Los Angeles papers, and the story was headline news for a week. The investigation was headed by the FBI because a religious institution was involved and there had previously been several incidents of a similar nature.

SCENE OF THE EXPLOSION THAT KILLED 10. In the aftermath of the explosion at the Fountain of the World headquarters, Ventura County coroner Virgil Payton (in white T-shirt) and firefighters pull another body from the rubble. Ten commune members died in the blast. As can be seen from this photograph taken the next morning after the 1:30 a.m. explosion, the multilevel structure was totally destroyed by the blast and resulting fire. The FBI later determined that the bomb was Gelignite, a high-grade military compound composed of 92 percent nitroglycerine.

MASTER KRISHNA VENTA (1911–1958). Krishna held a distinct resemblance to the popular images of Christ. Early after adopting the name Krishna, he claimed to be the "Risen Christ." In spite of the negatives, the WKFL helped many people during the years Krishna headed the Fountain of the World. They provided disaster assistance during fires, floods, and earthquakes; were trained in Red Cross First Aid; and had a trained corps of volunteer firefighters. The Fountain also provided assistance to battered women and homeless families.

VENTA, ALASKA. In 1956, Krishna journeyed north to Alaska by car with a small group of WKFL members to establish a second Fountain colony. Krishna had received permission under the Homestead Act to occupy three contiguous parcels of land at the head of Kachemak Bay near the Fox River, about 25 miles south of Homer on the Kenai Peninsula. The new settlement was called Venta, and the Fountain members were soon called "the Barefooters." This shows the homestead in 1958 where the Fountain members established their second colony.

WILBUR FOSTER YATES. Patriarch Wilbur was the Fountain elder and was drawn to Krishna because both shared a deep interest in philosophy. At the time of the Box Canyon bombing, he was 80 years old. Years earlier, Yates had been aligned with the Mormon religion, and in 1946, he authored a book titled *Master Passion*. The book drew from 20 years of writings by Yates and was a philosophical interpretation into the lost and hidden secrets of the Inner Self.

BISHOP NEKONA. Prior to joining the Fountain, Neva Booth taught school in Denver, Colorado. She met Krishna when he was on a lecture tour and came to Box Canyon in 1951 where her name was changed to Nekona. She quickly rose to the position of bishop and assumed a leadership role. Nekona was one of the few to survive the Box Canyon explosion and was sleeping not more than 30 feet from where the bomb was detonated. She led the Fountain in Box Canyon after Krishna's death into the mid-1960s.

PRIESTESS MARY. Mary Janet Meyer was an actress living in New York City when she first encountered the robed and barefooted Master Krishna in Times Square. She was in a bookstore searching titles in the theosophical section and felt immediately drawn to Krishna's aura. She followed him to California where she became a dedicated member of the Fountain and was very successful at soliciting donations for the group from the Hollywood film community.

BIBLIOGRAPHY

Cameron, Janet Scott. *Simi Grows Up, the Story of Simi*. Ventura County, CA: Anderson, Ritchie, and Simon, 1963.
Cornett, Frank M. *Recollections of a Pioneer Cowboy*. Simi, CA: Simi for Service, 1962.
Ehrheart, William J. *The World's Most Famous Movie Ranch*. Ventura, CA: Ventura County Historical Society Quarterly, Vol. 43, 1999.
Gebhard, David, Harriette VonBreton, and Robert W. Winter. *Samuel and Joseph Cather Newsom, Victorian Architectural Imagery in California 1878–1908*. Santa Barbara, CA: Regents of the University of California, 1979.
Haig, Gerald. *Straw Roads, a Story of Simi Valley from 1908 to 1960*. Simi Valley, CA: Simi Valley Historical Society, 1975.
Harrington, Robert E. *Early Days of Simi Valley*. Simi, CA: Alert Letter Shop, 1961.
Havens, Patricia, and Bill Appleton. *Simi Valley, a Journey Through Time*. Simi Valley, CA: Simi Valley Historical Society and Museum, 1997.
Hine, Robert V. *California's Utopian Colonies*. San Marino, CA: The Huntington Library, 1953.
Kagan, Paul. *New World Utopias, a Photographic History of the Search for Community*. New York, NY: Penguin Books, 1975.
Michel, D. L. "The Unholy Cult of the Great Sixth Seal," *Real Detective Magazine*. New York, NY: August 1932: 30–35.
Miller, Crane S. *The Changing Agricultural Landscape of the Simi Valley from 1795 to 1960*. Ventura, CA: Ventura County Historical Society Quarterly, Vol. 13, 1968.
Outland, Charles F. *Stagecoaching on El Camino Real, Los Angeles to San Francisco 1861–1901*. Glendale, CA: Arthur H. Clark Company, 1975.
Prisbrey, Tressa L. *Grandma Prisbrey's Bottle Village*. Simi Valley, CA: Preserve Bottle Village, 1998.
Schneider, Jerry L. *The Definitive True History of the Ray "Crash" Corrigan Movie Ranch*. Rialto, CA: Corriganville Press, 2007.
Thompson, Thomas H., and Albert Augustus. *West, History of Santa Barbara and Ventura Counties, California*. Oakland, CA: Thompson and West, 1883.

Visit us at
arcadiapublishing.com